Lead with, Courage! Narmen

Deborah L. Chima
2005

Choose To Lead

Advice, Tools, and Strategies
for Women from Women

Narmen Fennoy Hunter
Deborah Chambers Chima

05 06 07 08 09 HH 5 4 3 2 1
First Edition
Printed in the United States of America
ISBN 10: 0-9744149-7-2
ISBN 13: 978-09744149-7-2
BUS071000 Business & Economics/Leadership
Library of Congress Control Number: 2005920248

Requests for permission to make copies of any part of this work can be made to:

Cameo Publications, LLC.
PO Box 8006
Hilton Head Island, SC 29938
1-866-372-2636
www.cameopublications.com
info@cameopublications.com

The cover and interior layout were designed by
David Josephson, CTM, of Cameo Publications, LLC.

From Narmen Fennoy Hunter:
This book is dedicated to my mother, Gladys Stennis Fennoy, and my grandmother, Lena McDonald Fennoy, who led with, vision, values, purpose, and love; to my father, William Fennoy, Jr., and my grandfathers, William Fennoy, Sr. and Howard Stennis, who treated my three brothers and my sister and me the same; and to women who, with their leadership, can change the world.

From Deborah Chambers Chima:
In memory of my mother Rosetta Chambers-Smith, who demanded nothing less than excellence. I miss you daily.

In memory of my son, Michael Angelo Chima.

Contents

Contents

ACKNOWLEDGMENTS

Choose to Lead—Advice, Tools, and Strategies for Women from Women has been a joint project from the beginning. We take this opportunity to acknowledge all of those who have supported our efforts in this first publication. The support and encouragement has been so important during the times when we wondered if and when we would get to the last page. We are especially grateful to the many women who made the time in their busy schedules to share with us their success tips and stories. These tips and stories were shared in the hope that other women would find them useful on their leadership journey.

We also want to thank Dawn Josephson, our editor and David Josephson, our publisher at Cameo Publications, LLC.

From Narmen Fennoy Hunter

Let me first acknowledge God and his awesome presence in my life. He has made all of this possible. It has been an eye-opening experience collaborating with Deborah on this book project. Jointly writing was a baby idea we had in 2003. Finally, in 2004 we decided to just do it. We have worked many days, late nights, early mornings, and many weekends to bring this book to publication. We have been excited, laughed, and groaned as we've gone through several iterations of the chapters. Deborah has been a very focused and resourceful partner, and a great friend through it all. Thank You.

Thank you, Dan Coughlin, my coach, for your unswerving encouragement for me to write. At different times during the project, I had to call on family and friends for contact information for some of the contributors to this book. I appreciate all of your assistance. Thank you Will Lew for your recommendations and for making the initial contact. I acknowlege a group of women who came together at a critical point in time and led with courage, vision, and determination: Annette, Chere', Cheryl, Danitra, Janann, Michelle, Michelle, and Pat. Amy, Erica, and Staci continue to lead.

To Larine Cowan, Clara Crowell, and Norma Willis, my friends for longer than I will tell, thank you for always being there, and for the fun and stories we have shared over the years.

To my best friend and sister, Carmen Moody, who has always been one of my strongest supporters, thank you. To my brothers William,

Nino, and Lovell Fennoy, thank you for your encouragement and belief in me. Thank you Bernice Bellamy for your support and the hours you spent reading and checking with red pen in hand. To my son Chaunsey—I love and appreciate you. Thank you for understanding and laughing at my humor. To my grandchildren Andrew, Ashton, Ryan, and Langston who are my reality check, you bring so much love, fun and fresh perspective to my life.

To the women of my family (past) thank you for your legacy of spirit, vision, tenacity, and accomplishment; to the young women of my family (present), your contributions are unfolding, and to the little girls of my family, the future belongs to you; claim it.

From Deborah Chambers Chima

First, giving honor to God from whom all blessings flow. To my entire family, especially my big sister, Vivian Chambers, who has always supported me unconditionally for as long as I can remember. I love you. To my aunts, Leana Phillips and Lizzie Adams, who in their 90s continue to be role models of what it means to be strong women who don't compromise their values.

To both of my mentors, Narmen Fennoy Hunter and Jylla Moore Foster. Narmen, in the twenty years we have been friends, you have always believed in my skills and desire to make things happen. Thank you for all of the hours you spent coaching me to my destiny. Thank you for your patience in letting me grow my way. Jylla, you were the first to help me see that I truly could make the leap to creating my future. Your guidance and council will always be needed and appreciated.

To my business coach, Sylva Leduc, who did not hesitate to share her network and all of her business acumen.

To the two bosses, Jack Berry and Valentino Reefer, who were most instrumental in shaping my management style. Thanks for believing in me.

To my Pastor, Rev. Jesse Hawkins, Jr., of St. John AME Church, Aurora. It is under your ministry that I have received the spiritual knowledge that gave me the courage to step out on faith.

To all my sister girlfriends, the few people who call me Deb because you have known me for so long. Much love to Pat, Gail, Terry, Joyce, Shawn, Regina, Melody, Linda, and Toni Flo. It has been quite a journey so far, and we will see each other through till the end.

Finally, to Willie Gartrell, thanks for the laughs and lessons. Friends Forever.

Foreword

S uccessful leadership is all about the people. I work in one of the most technologically advanced industries in the world. But success for us isn't found in the technology—it's in the people. Everyday you must live and lead in a manner that illustrates you genuinely care. You must not only require results, but also, you must show that you care about those in the field trying to deliver them. Over the years I have interacted with many women in leadership positions and admired their skills in developing people.

One of my early mentors is the retired Vice President of Customer Service for Ameritech (later acquired by SBC). Her name is Rita Reed and her leadership style was such that her people would "run through a brick wall" to meet her goals. Most of us don't need that kind of loyalty, but it clearly takes outstanding leadership skills to get that type of response from your organization. Why did they do that? Because she showed she cared.

Another role model for me is Krista Tillman, President of North Carolina Operations for Bell South. In her office hangs a sign that reads "What do you recommend?" She empowers her team and has created an environment where they are free to make suggestions about how to solve problems. She confirms that the best leaders ask more questions and give fewer orders.

These women are examples of how women in leadership roles use their influence to achieve results. Their style of management encompasses team building, leveraging diversity, effective communication, people development, and change leadership, which are the five leadership competencies discussed in this book. I fully embrace the concept of more women learning to improve their leadership skills. I encourage more women to pick up the leadership mantle. Use your talents to the fullest. We all win when you do.

Deon Bradley
Vice President
Bell South

Choose To Lead

Advice, Tools, and Strategies
for Women from Women

Narmen Fennoy Hunter
Deborah Chambers Chima

Chapter One:

Introduction

C hoosing to lead is a conscious act. Falling into leadership is not. Choosing to lead sets a process in motion for reaching your goals. Choosing to lead and moving strategically in that goal direction, along with the appropriate advice and tools, can catapult you to the next level.

Too many women fall into leadership roles by chance rather than choosing to lead. In our conversations with several women in leadership positions, we learned that some had not set a course for leadership, and had not prepared themselves early in their careers. Consequently, it may have taken them longer to get to the positions they now hold. They may have experienced unnecessary setbacks. They may not have developed the networks that could have provided the formal and informal relationships to help them in their leadership quest. One executive vice president indicated that she did not know any women who had made the conscious choice to lead. She said, "we kind of make it to leadership positions and do the best we can when we get there to make it work".

Our purpose is to see more women make the conscious choice to lead.

This book is for every woman who has ever given the slightest thought to making a difference by changing something to make it better. And what woman hasn't? This book is for women who want to learn more about leadership before choosing to lead; women who want to serve as coaches or mentors; women who want to lead but don't know how; women who have never considered leading because they think it is too difficult; and women who have experienced leading and are seeking guidance to be more effective. It is also for the men who would dare to read a leadership development book written for women by women. The target audience for this book is women. However, the competencies for effective leadership are universal. We therefore invite men who want to be more effective leaders to read about and use the tools that we have provided. We want to take this opportunity to help men better understand the issues that confront women who choose to lead, and how men can better support and facilitate the leadership development process of women.

In today's economy of downsizing and flatter organizations, more emphasis on team performance, and with more than 50% of the workforce being female, women leaders are needed. What should be even more glass-ceiling shattering is this statement, by Tom Peters, "My 'business' is haranguing business leaders about my fact-based conviction that women's increasing power—leadership skills and purchasing power—is the Strongest and Most Dynamic Force at Work in the American Economy today."

Women control most consumer purchases:
+ All consumer purchases: 83%.
+ Home furnishings: 94%.
+ Vacations: 92%.
+ New homes: 91%.
+ Do It Yourself home projects: 80%.
+ Consumer Electronics: 51%.
+ Cars: 60%. (…women significantly influence another 30% of the purchases, bringing their power score to 90 %.)

The same pattern holds in services:
+ New bank accounts: women make the choice 89% of the time.
+ Healthcare: women make 80% of decisions, and are responsible for about two-thirds of spending.

*Source: Tom Peters, *Re-imagine!,* 2004

> ✦ American women write 80% of all checks, pay 61% of all
> bills, and own 53% of all stock.
>
> ✦ American women constitute 43% of Americans with a net
> worth of a half-million dollars or more, influencing 75% of
> financial decisions.
>
> *Source: Tom Peters, *Re-imagine!*, 2004

By 2005, 4.7 million women will be self-employed. In her book, *EVEolution*, Faith Popcorn indicates that "women start businesses at twice the rate of men (every sixty seconds), ..." "Female-owned and female-run businesses generate $3.6 trillion annually and employ 27.5 million people—more than all the Fortune 500 companies combined, in America." This means that the revenue from female-owned and run business is more than the Gross Domestic Product (GDP) of Germany.

Organizations that want to lead in their industry, know and understand the importance of the female market and its direct and indirect impact on their business.

It follows that these organizations need to make it a priority to develop and promote the female leadership capabilities within their organizations. Women who want to lead should seize this moment of opportunity for development, mentoring, being mentored and the mentoring of others.

What is Leadership?

Leadership is the art of getting things done through people. We, like you, have often wondered what it takes for this dimension to shine throughout the fabric of our lives. Most people tend to see leadership as standing out at specific times and not necessarily like a thread holding our entire life fabric together. In our approach to the topic, we define leadership very broadly, because any environment or situation provides the opportunity for women to play a leadership role.

Leadership is critical at this time in both our personal and professional lives. With the many corporate scandals that we have heard and read much about, the public continues to ask "What does it take to lead?" After all, people made the decisions and took the actions that created the corporate scandals—individuals who were in senior leadership positions. Leaders have the responsibility to lead with vision, ethics, and the interests of the organization and its employees, and stockholders as top priorities.

As we discuss leadership throughout this book, the reference is to *effective and ethical* leadership.

So many components and styles of leadership exist. You may feel confused on which theory or model to follow. Have you ever wished for a definitive understanding of leadership and the requisite skills to which you can relate and immediately put into action from a woman's perspective? That is one of the purposes of this book. We will also provide insightful advice, leadership tools and strategies.

Throughout the book we will address leadership—its importance and its impact on you and those you are leading, as well as, approaches on learning to lead and leading well. Specifically, we address consciously choosing to lead, and the how-to and results of effective leadership. To that end, we have identified five essential competencies for effective leadership. They are:

1. Team Building

2. Leveraging Diversity

3. Communication

4. Leading Change

5. People Development

We will discuss how each of these competencies builds leadership capability.

We describe, in a step-by-step manner, proven techniques for learning and mastering these five competencies. We write about networking as an important skill to learn and use. Networking, done the most effective way, grows relationships, is two way, and serves you in many situations and over many years. *Choose to Lead* identifies some of the obstacles to leading and how to prevent and remove the obstacles. Women will know the importance of a mentor and how to select one or many. They will learn strategies for dealing with that age-old problem of being heard while in a meeting with a group of males.

We will share with you some of our 'lessons learned' on this leadership journey. We will also share the experiences of twenty-seven women from seven different career paths:

1. Academia/Education

2. Business/Corporate

3. Community

4. Entrepreneurial

5. Government/Politics

6. Philanthropy

7. Religion

Some of the names will be familiar; others will be new to you.

We have also provided leadership interactive exercises. This is an opportunity for you to apply the advice, tools, and strategies that you have read. It is an additional learning feature that makes the approach used in *Choose to Lead* different and valuable.

We will equip you with the information you can use to grow and thrive in your current leadership role or assist you in your quest to take on the leadership role(s) to which you aspire. Most important to note is that you can learn to lead, and you can be a more effective leader as you read and understand how other leaders think, act, and interact. As a result of this book, we hope you will craft an actionable leadership plan designed to take you to your next level of success.

The shoe prints throughout the book denote key points.

Chapter Two:
Identifying the Leadership Gaps

M any times current leaders do not pass the leadership gauntlet to deserving women due to the unspoken concern about whether women can remain focused on the business of the organization. The issue of work and life balance continues to dominate the discussion of women being ready for leadership roles. "Can she effectively manage home and work?" is a common question. Too often, the female style of leadership (questioning, supportive, and inclusive) is so misunderstood that decision-makers shy away from placing women in strategic roles.

A leadership gap occurs as women hold back when they really have what it takes to lead. They may be uncomfortable leading, feeling that a team of males will respond inappropriately or female teammates will not embrace them. They may be straddling the fence, not sure if leading is the role they want to play. Women may feel that the organization's culture is not supportive of women in leadership roles. Whatever the reason, potential leaders who hold back waste much time, and the organization loses potential contributions in the form of new ideas, approaches, and solutions.

Women have so much to offer in the area of leadership. Yet a significant gap exists between women who are at the top of their game, demonstrating and executing leadership, and women who have aspirations but just can't make it happen. Why does this gap exist? *It comes down to a matter of choices and a strategic focus.* Women who are achieving their goal to be a respected leader, make conscious choices on a regular basis. They choose to weave their leadership threads strategically.

23

Take a look at this story. Alicia has aspirations to move up the corporate ladder. She is always eager to assist her department with achieving their goals. Yet during the meetings, she either gets cut off when speaking, or someone else on the team picks up on her good ideas and winds up getting the credit.

Ann also has management aspirations. She too is eager to assist her department. She wants her peers to see her as a leader. When she receives the meeting agenda, she takes the time to think about how she can contribute to the discussion. Ann knows the importance of talking with the decision-makers before the actual meeting. She then networks with trusted members of her team and shares her ideas. She effectively communicates how her ideas benefit the team. This way, prior to the meeting she has received feedback and gained support. As a result, others accept and implement her ideas. Ann is more strategic than Alicia because she is proactive, takes action, and is prepared. She seizes the opportunity to weave the thread of leadership.

Like Alicia, you may have great ideas and contributions yet lack the know-how to demonstrate effective leadership in getting support and recognition for those ideas. Therefore, you need to discuss and get buy-in from key persons for your ideas prior to the meeting. When you are presenting your ideas to the group, do not allow others to interrupt your idea presentation. Continue to confidently present your ideas. Others will soon get the message and wait until you have completed your presentation.

Demonstrating Leadership

Leadership is the ability to provide the vision and persuade others to follow. Do you know how to demonstrate leadership?

▶▶Leadership behaviors look like this:

☒ Use of effective verbal and written communication includes timely communication to the appropriate people.

☒ The necessary planning and budget are made available for people development.

☒ Team building is championed, recognized, and rewarded.

☒ Diversity is leveraged to achieve the best thinking and highest performance. It is understood as a business necessity, as well as, the right thing to do.

☒ Change is embraced and led as a result of understanding the short and long range goals of the organization.

Are you caught up in displaying non-leadership behaviors and looking for a way to end the cycle?

· ➤
· ➤**Non-leadership behaviors looks like this:**

☒ Choosing not to communicate or communicating ineffectively and in an untimely manner.

☒ Rejecting the need for people development or funding it at inadequate levels.

☒ Not encouraging or supporting team building.

☒ Refusing to concede when the team doesn't choose your ideas.

☒ Verbally agreeing to an idea yet not making an effort to contribute to its success.

☒ Leveraging diversity is only talk with no support or action.

☒ Denial that change will happen and not being ready when it does.

These are only a few examples. When you find yourself displaying these non-leadership behaviors, remind yourself to change the behavior to leadership behavior.

Closing the Gaps

We identified the gaps as: 1) women holding back when they have what it takes to lead, and 2) the difference between women who demonstrate effective leadership and those who aspire to lead but just can't make it happen. Begin to close these gaps to prepare yourself by determining what is important to you. Decide what you will or will not do as you travel this path, and begin working to get what you want.

Make a plan to address any of your deficiencies. Anticipate the next opportunity to network. Be ready to work at getting the position you desire. You may even be able to create your next opportunity.

Do you feel that you are in the race alone and no one really understands your issues? Some women can be so sensitive that they isolate themselves and feel that they are on an island. Don't let your emotions cause you to miss the opportunity to weave your leadership threads. When you begin to have thoughts of isolation you must immediately refocus. Another option always exists. Focus your energy on identifying people resources with whom you can relate. The quicker you are able to adapt your thinking, the faster you will attract people who want to hear what you have to say.

Like many women, you may even feel overwhelmed and/or frustrated. The items on your to do list never seem to end. You continue to work excessively long hours trying to get the leadership role. You may even lack a sufficient support system to assist you in fulfilling your leadership dreams and desires. If these are issues that confront you, be aware that we will address them.

When you think that you are getting mired in the muck of executing day-to-day responsibilities, ask yourself this question: "Do I have the skills or resources to identify the best solutions for pulling myself out of the muck cycle in a timely manner?" Remember that if you do get mired, you must first have the awareness that you are stuck. Only then can you begin to identify either what you personally need to do differently or whom you need to ask for help. Let's continue to look at opportunities for getting prepared to lead and closing the gaps.

We know that both internal and external barriers prevent women from achieving leadership roles. The internal barriers are those that are self-imposed. Normally you can directly control and eliminate them. One of the most common internal barriers is self-doubt—lacking confidence in your own abilities. Another is continually second-guessing yourself when you make a decision. Doing so makes you appear weak. Other relevant internal barriers are: undeveloped networking skills, unwilling to pursue opportunities, undeveloped communication skills, uncomfortable speaking in public, unable to verbalize the organization's vision, purpose, mission, and goals, and non-alignment of your actionable goals with those of your department and organization. The external barriers are those that are imposed by others. Some of the most common external barriers are: racism, sexism, and lack of organizational support for mentoring. You can stay in the fight for leadership roles and not lose your momentum despite these barriers.

The fact remains that women can thrive as leaders by acknowledging these and other barriers, and developing solutions to overcome them. Not only is it possible, but it is imperative for women to position themselves successfully so they can demonstrate their leadership abilities. With the appropriate training, mentoring, personal growth, and opportunities, women can develop into effective leaders. For those who are ready to lead now, begin to use the threads of leadership and weave the fabric that you envision.

Rest assured you'll have many opportunities for dress rehearsal prior to the main leadership event. These opportunities exist in the corporate environment as well as in non-corporate environments— within the church, schools, government, politics, philanthropy, and the community. Volunteering to chair a committee that is working on a highly visible project can be a way to learn how to move your ideas through an agenda. Another opportunity is joining a community organization and volunteering to take on a task that could strategically take the organization to the next level. Take advantage of these and other dress rehearsal leadership opportunities.

Honing your leadership skills outside the work environment is an ideal way to practice. Decide now where you want to lead and do it. Start wherever you are as you prepare for what you consider being the 'real' leadership live performance. You can be the leader you aspire to be. For some it appears to be an inborn dimension. For most it is a learned skill. Think of leadership as the thread and opportunities as the fabric. Create your path one stitch at a time. Before you realize it, you will have created a leadership mosaic tapestry that is respected and coveted.

We've asked questions and provided some answers. We have done this purposefully to let you know that we are aware of the issues that you face. In other chapters we will provide you with more answers in the form of advice, tools, and strategies. Through our collective leadership experiences and those of our invited contributors, we will assist you in reaching your leadership goals. With this book we make it easy for you to begin to weave the threads of leadership throughout your personal and professional lives.

Chapter Three:

Making a Difference in Your Personal and Professional Lives

W hether you are driven with a sense of purpose to lead or still seeking a leadership pattern that fits you, you likely understand and value the importance of leadership. As you better understand the significance of choosing to lead and the importance of demonstrating leadership, you will be able to identify opportunities where your leadership will make a difference in your life as well as that of others. Remember, you can have all of the talent and ability required to be a leader, yet you must still choose to lead.

Consciously or not, women weave their leadership abilities into their daily tasks at home, work, and in the community. Our ability to multi-task is a part of who we are as women. This innate skill is one of the many reasons why we need to have more women in leadership roles. In this chapter we discuss:

- ☒ roles
- ☒ making a difference in your personal and professional lives through leadership
- ☒ effectively demonstrating leadership

A number of factors influence your choice to lead. These factors can impact your personal and professional lives.

· ►Five of the major factors influencing your decisions are:

1. Family
2. Religion
3. Education
4. Gender
5. Race

These factors have influenced you all of your life—both consciously and unconsciously. They were even at play before you were born as your parent(s) decided the colors of your room, your bassinet, and clothes when bringing you from the hospital. Your toys and games, your family interactions, your neighbors and friends all have significantly influenced you.

Generally, boys are raised to be more aggressive and leadership focused, whereas girls are raised to be supporters and tend to keep the playing field level and less focused on leadership. They are more team oriented. Boys grow into men who seek opportunities to demonstrate leadership, whereas girls grow into women who tend to wait to be asked to take on a leadership role.

Your perceptions about life and people developed at a very early age. Unless modified or changed, these perceptions continue to determine how you view yourself, the organization and your role, the extent to which you value the diversity of your co-workers, the way in which you interact with them, and the degree to which you choose, or, not choose to enable their growth and development within the organization.

In the book *Our Separate Ways—Black and White Women and the Struggle for Professional Identity*, Ella Bell and Stella Nkomo discuss the influence of family, education, religion, gender, and race on our personal and professional choices. Black women, as they climb in the organization, expect to use their talent, skills, and education to help others. "Their personal mobility is experienced as part of the mobility of their whole group." On the other hand, white women are more likely to feel that they fit into the corporation and that the playing field is equal for anyone who chooses to play—a more individualistic course. In order for more women to achieve leadership status, it takes visible mentoring and supportive alliances between women. Men, many times, won't give women an opportunity. If women are not willing to give other women the leadership opportunities, who will?

The leadership threads of both your personal and professional lives weave together. Your personal life choices are determined by what is important to you, what you want to achieve, when and how you will achieve it, and what you are willing to do to get it. It is not as simple as it may sound. We do, however, offer steps that will help you identify how to lead in both your personal and professional lives.

► The steps are:

✦ **Step One:** Determine what is important to you—what matters most. This first step gives direction for the next four steps. Set specific, measurable, achievable, and realistic goals with time frames to provide focus, clarity, and direction. So for you, 'what matters most' may be chairing a committee, getting promoted to the next level, or starting a family. Your goals could also be balancing family, community, and work. Be realistic in setting time frames for completing your goals. Take into consideration what needs to be done to reach the goal, and your other responsibilities.

✦ **Step Two:** Prioritize your goals. Determine the order in which you want to achieve the goals you have identified for yourself. This goes back to Step One—determining what matters most. For instance, if you have three goals—a promotion, starting a family, and chairing the local political action committee—ask yourself which matters most. This decision will determine the priority order.

✦ **Step Three:** Determine action plans with time parameters for reaching each goal. As with your goals, you must also prioritize action plans. Make sure that the action plans are aligned with the goals. Many times we are working on various projects and activities that have little to do with the goals we have set. Execution or following through on the action plans is critical to your success.

✦ **Step Four:** Design a way to track your progress. Determine at key intervals whether you are on track. If you are, keep going. If you are not, determine your options and change directions. You may use either an electronic gadget, pen and paper or both. You may want to use calendar tracking or some other type of visual aide. Use whatever method works for you as long as you track your progress.

✦ **Step Five:** Determine a way to measure the achievement of your goals. At the end of the day, you need to answer the question: "Did I reach my goal? Again, this goes back to Step One. If you were specific in writing your goals, you know what to measure.

You can more easily say no to distractions or anything that takes you off track when you have a greater yes. The greater yes is knowing where you are going, why, and when you want to get there. The greater yes is having goals that lead and direct your life. We encourage you to weave the fabric that creates your own greater yes opportunities.

To further reinforce the point of the relationship between your choice to lead personally and professionally, let's take a look at this example. Suppose you work for a large and prestigious company. You are in senior management, working sixty to seventy hours a week, and have a husband and children. You are trying to balance several major projects at the office. You are also very active in your community and your church. You want to do it all, even though you hardly have time to breathe. Recently your doctor advised you to slow down. You are wondering how you can possibly do that. You feel that everything and everyone around you is leading your life. You seem to have no control over what is happening. If you feel this way, you probably omitted the first step in the process that we discussed earlier.

Let's look at how you can redirect your life by following the five steps outlined above. Perhaps you need to go back to step one and determine 'what matters most' to you. What are your goals and your priorities?

As you determine what is important to you and what matters most, consider redirecting your energies. For example, in your personal life, perhaps you can delay the community work until later in the year. Also, work with your spouse to make alternative arrangements for picking up and dropping off the children. As for the numerous projects at the office, remember that although you are trying to move ahead, you cannot say 'yes' to every major project. Take the time to reassess the importance of your projects. Determine how they can be completed by either working through others or reassigning the total project.

Determine whether you need to renegotiate the time lines. If so, do it now. Do not wait until the project due date. Take a look at how you are using your time throughout the day. In addition, find more ways to work smarter rather than harder by making use of current and available technology. By taking these actions you are following steps one, two, and three. Choose to lead in your personal and professional lives with prioritized goals based on what matters most and aligned action plans. This is your greater yes. The goals and action plans provide the clarity and focus for you to say yes to actions and activities that support your goals and no to distractions that take you off track.

Making Hard Decisions

Making hard decisions about what is important to you and your success and then acting on those decisions is taking leadership. Leading is taking ownership—ownership of making something happen that you envision. This does not mean being the Lone Ranger. Remember that you need others to help you reach your desired level of success. As people begin to trust that you are a team player and not the Lone Ranger, they will be more open to assisting you. Being successful includes inspiring and helping others be successful as they participate in making the vision come to life. No matter what your past leadership experience, the following strategies will help you.

Leading For the First Time

☒ Choose well-respected and positioned leaders to be your mentors. It is to your advantage to have more than one mentor. You might have one whose strength is strategic thinking and another whose strength is knowledge of the organization and its key players. You might consider a leader whose strength is relationship building or networking.

☒ Identify and focus on the department or project goals and communicate them clearly to those with whom you are working.

☒ Identify key people and make yourself available for feedback opportunities.

☒ Find the most supportive environment you can. Professional associations are always seeking individuals who are willing to share their expertise. This environment is usually a more flexible one in which to develop your leadership skills.

☒ On a challenging assignment, have the support of your supervisor. This helps ensure success. Be prepared to communicate how you plan to be successful in reaching your goals. Most supervisors will support your desire to demonstrate leadership as long as you can articulate how your efforts support the department's or organization's goals.

Experienced in Demonstrating Leadership

☒ Focus on choosing strategic opportunities on the job or in the community that will provide you the exposure needed to reach your next development goal.

☒ Assess your past accomplishments and failures and identify trends.

☒ Take the time to list the opportunities where your past accomplishments will be the catalyst for you being viewed as the leader of choice.

☒ In the chairperson or team leader position, develop ways that you can take the committee or team to a high level of execution.

☒ Match your unique skill sets to a problem area where you know you will be successful.

Courage and Risk-taking

You have probably seen women who look and sound confident and at ease—no matter where they are or what they are doing. How do these women do it? Normally it is because they are successful at what they do, and they are leading in their personal and professional lives. You can have that same air of confidence when you lead in your personal and professional life.

Remember, choosing to lead involves courage and risk taking, and taking risks improves self-confidence. Improved self-confidence leads to more effective performance. More effective performance leads to realized vision and achieved goals, and a visible sense of confidence and ease.

➤Feedback

Demonstrating leadership is being open to feedback and being prepared for others to critique you relentlessly. So be willing to hear all types of feedback. Some messages will be positive and enriching and some will be negative and demoralizing. Listen to the content of the feedback. If you question whether the negative feedback is valid, ask a person you trust to give their honest opinion. The bottom line is, do not discount the feedback simply because you don't agree with it. You can learn from every situation.

Attitudes

Your attitude about who you are and what you bring to the table is critical. Do not try to demonstrate leadership by thinking you are invincible or worse yet, a know it all. Never compare yourself to others. Too often women limit their potential because they are too worried about the competition. Instead, focus your energy on defining your strengths and then identifying areas where you can demonstrate your skills. Your uniqueness makes you stand out in a crowd, not your ability to emulate what someone else is doing. It is okay to think about how your style could accommodate desired behaviors that you have observed in someone else. The danger zone lies in trying to display a leadership style that doesn't fit you. You will confuse yourself and others, thus diluting your leadership attempt.

Being Perfect

Leaders are not perfect. The desire to be perfect gets us mired in the muck. Don't dwell on the error. Rather, learn to deal with mishandled assignments or negative interactions with someone and move on. Start the new day with a fresh mindset, and don't be too hard on yourself. Our desire to be credible creates an emotional toll when things don't go right. Don't let anyone make you feel inadequate. If you need to apologize to someone, do so sincerely. Don't be concerned about how you will be viewed if you think the apology is going to help you refocus.

We've provided you with a process for choosing to lead, as well as advice and strategies on how to effectively demonstrate leadership. In Chapter Two, we introduced Ann and Alicia. Take a look at this story as we continue their leadership journey.

Alicia and Ann both desire to be viewed as leaders. Alicia notices that Ann always gets the high profile assignments. She believes she can also do a great job but when she compares herself to Ann, her confidence wavers. In the past, Alicia became stressed when she received feedback from the team regarding a project in which she served as the team leader. She wants the chance to prove herself again but she can't seem to forget her past mistakes. She is convinced that the boss is not supportive of her career goals because she never gets assignments that provide high visibility like Ann does. So she decides to try to act more like Ann during the team meetings by raising her hand more often. Her goal is to get attention, yet as the other team members begin to question her ideas, she feels that she is being attacked. She gets flustered and reacts negatively to the team members. Alicia has allowed her fear of failure to deter her from reaching her career goals. She goes home each evening and complains to her family about how she is not valued at work. Her choices have not led to her goal of being viewed as a leader.

On the other hand, Ann is confident in her ability to get results. Whenever possible, she seeks opportunities to lead. When she wants to lead a challenging project that will stretch her skills, she meets with the boss to communicate her thoughts on why she would be the best person for the lead job. She outlines her strengths and has well thought out answers as to how she will overcome obstacles. When the team challenges her ideas during the meetings, she listens and responds without emotion. If she makes a mistake, she acknowledges it and tries to find humor in the situation. She always gives credit to others if someone else fixes the mistake. If a team member asks her a question she can't answer, she polls the team to determine if someone else can respond. Ann volunteers to get the answer by the end of the day if the answer cannot be determined during the meeting. She does not allow the fact that she didn't know something deter her from leading the rest of the meeting. With the accomplishment of each challenging goal, her confidence soars. As a result, she becomes more focused, and management views her as a high potential employee. When she goes home to her family she is able to spend quality time with them whenever possible. Ann courageously demonstrates leadership and does not allow the possibility of failure to deter her from her career goals.

Ann's decision to lead has positively impacted her personal and professional life. Like her, you need to determine what is important to you and act on it. Do not let anything or anyone get you off track. In the event you do, refocus on what matters most and start again.

Chapter Four:

How Effective Leaders Do What They Do

In most instances, the ability to lead people did not happen overnight and not without some pain, recrimination, and self-examination. Effective leaders do what they do because they have a history of three things:

1. They take the time to know themselves.

2. They know how to get things done through people.

3. They execute their action plans, and hence accomplish their goals.

1. Effective leaders take the time to know themselves.

☒ They know their own strengths and weaknesses.

☒ They focus on their strengths and have learned to manage their weaknesses.

☒ They know their own work style and behavior patterns.

☒ They surround themselves with diverse people whose ideas, work styles, and behavior patterns complement theirs.

☒ They know where they want to go.

☒ They are self-motivated and confident they will reach their goals.

Strategies To Consider

☒ Use your available resources to begin or continue the process of determining your strengths and weaknesses. Many organizations provide opportunities for your personal and professional growth and development. Find out what programs or services your organization offers that will assist you in the process of determining your strengths and weaknesses. Your human resources department can provide information on available assessment feedback instruments your organization uses. In some of our client organizations the 360-degree assessment tool is popular, where your peers, subordinates, and of course your boss provide input on your strengths and weaknesses. Be sure to let people know that you also want recommendations for improvements.

☒ The performance review process is also an opportunity to determine your success areas and other areas that need some attention. A key to addressing the identified areas is to write a plan for making the appropriate changes in performance and/or behavior. In some organizations, your customers are also asked to provide input on your performance. Informally, you can ask a colleague whom you respect to provide feedback on your strengths and weaknesses. Listen. Be open to receiving the feedback. Thank them for taking the time to give their input.

☒ Outside the work setting, ask close friends whom you respect to comment on how you do the things with which they are familiar. Be open to receiving the feedback. Listen and don't try to defend why or how you do what you do. Thank them for being open and honest.

·➤ ➡ 2. Effective leaders know how to get things done through people.

☒ They know that people are their most valuable asset in reaching their goals.

☒ They understand the importance of having people involved at various levels in the visioning, goal setting, and strategy development processes.

☒ They have mastered the art of getting people to see the vision, participate in goal setting, and determine the strategy and actionable plan.

☒ They recognize, support, develop, and reward people.

Seeing the larger vision of the organization and the goals that support the vision, helps mobilize people around a common focus. As people participate in determining the strategy, they identify the how-to and the who-will-do for reaching the goals.

·➤ ➡ 3. Effective leaders know the importance of execution in reaching their goals.

☒ They set and align key actions to goals.

☒ They stay focused on the action plan.

☒ They communicate, communicate, and communicate around the action plan.

☒ They execute the action plan.

☒ They follow up, track, and measure.

By remaining focused on the execution of the aligned plan, effective leaders set the standard for doing what is necessary to reach predetermined goals.

In Chapter One we have identified the five essential competencies for effective leadership as:

1. Communication

2. People Development

3. Team Building

4. Leveraging Diversity

5. Leading Change

In this chapter we will describe how effective leaders use these competencies to do what they do. First, let's take a look at Ann and how her skills in the competency areas impact the leadership style she uses.

Due to the results she has achieved, Ann is now on the fast track to reaching the coveted corner executive office. If you were to ask her how she accomplished this milestone, she would let you know that the smartest thing she has done is to surround herself with a team that supports her vision for the department. Her direct reports are loyal to her because she has consistently demonstrated her desire to see them reach their own career aspirations. She effectively communicates with each team member on a one-on-one basis to discuss how his or her goals achieve the bigger win for the team. She schedules time on a monthly basis to listen to and support each of the managers in the accomplishment of their goals. She allows them to determine the agenda for the meetings with the understanding that she will in turn give candid feedback on their progress.

Ann stays abreast of the latest information that might impact organizational changes to ensure that her team can make timely adjustments as needed. Her team looks forward to the development sessions because they know she is committed to assisting them in their professional growth. She gives appropriate and timely recognition for their progress. Her team trusts her because she has earned their trust. They know that with her, there is no hidden agenda. When she makes promises, she keeps them. Ann realizes that trust is the most important element for getting results through others, so she is careful to ensure she doesn't make a promise she can't keep. Her team knows that she will respond to their request in a reasonable period of time. Prior to adding new members, Ann strategically considers any skill gaps in the current team. To ensure the new employee is going to fit in, she schedules time prior to the hire for the team and the individual to be together. It's not just Ann's decision.

Ann is not perfect. Due to her ambitious career aspirations, she is very demanding of others in the area of achieving results. Her secret to keeping her team happy even when she is pushing them is to ensure that she consistently behaves the same way every day. Her direct reports know that when the pressure is on, Ann will become more vocal if she sees things moving too slowly. With rap sessions they have had on this topic, they now believe through her modified behavior that if she is coming on too strong, they need to communicate their uncomfortable feelings. Ann has demonstrated that she is okay with this type of feedback. Her team has learned that she has their best interest in mind even when she is under pressure.

If you aspire to be more like Ann, a leader who is appreciated and respected, focus on the following five essential competencies of leadership. In our discussion we will provide you with actionable strategies to consider as you create a vision of what you want your leadership style to be.

►Communication

Whether you desire to be viewed as a community leader, corporate executive, or prestigious board member, your communication style will ultimately determine how others perceive you. What and how you communicate shows what you know, how you feel, and how much you value someone or something. Communication is an integral part of your life—at home, at work, anywhere. Few people go through the day without some form of communication. The whole process of visioning, goal setting, strategy development, and execution of action plans takes communication. Whether communicating verbally or in written form, communication should be with focus and with clarity. What is your point? What do you want the listener to know and understand? Who is the audience and how much time do you have to convey the message? The whole process simply means "engage brain before opening mouth." Effective leaders know and understand the importance of communication. They communicate with the end in mind.

Communication is a matter of letting others know you are listening. That requires the ability to stop talking and be quiet. This is a challenge for most of us, especially as managers. We are usually trying to think of what to say next and miss the talker's point. People know when you are listening and when you are not listening. They see you looking around, fidgeting, and appearing preoccupied with other thoughts.

The feedback from Ann's team indicates that Ann has learned to listen to them. She is aware of their concerns and does what is necessary to resolve issues.

Listening includes knowing your audience and having the ability to hear the messages they are communicating to you. The message could be support for ideas presented, disagreement about process, eagerness to move on, or enthusiasm for successful endeavors.

How do effective leaders develop this communication capability? They practice on friends, family, peers, and strangers. When they volunteer they choose an organization where they must communicate, verbally or in written form. They may be a part of a Toastmasters' group. They may have taken a presentation skills class. They may have used a coach. They ask for their written work to be critiqued. They ask for feedback on meeting presentations. You need to be aware of the latest communication technology so that you can use it to communicate even more effectively. Some or all of these are ways you can improve your communication skills and style to help you be the leader you envision.

Like Ann, you understand that your word is your bond. What you say and commit to is what you must follow through on in order to gain the respect of others. A leader uses their communication skills to motivate people. This leadership competency is critical in helping others to reach their highest level of potential. Leaders make sure they are consistent when defining and communicating department and organizational expectations. This consistency ensures that everyone hears the same message. Challenge yourself to treat everyone you encounter with the same level of communication you expect from them. When you run into difficult people, be aware that your communication skills will be tested. It is better to table a discussion rather than allow your emotions to cause you to overreact. Women must be aware of the possibility of derailment when we don't stay in control of our emotions. No matter how unprofessional the other person may be in their communication style, don't get hooked.

When we communicate, women have to be aware of how our communication style impacts others. Men pride themselves on being analytical and able to succinctly communicate a message. Some women struggle with getting to the point and being able to clearly communicate how the message impacts others. If you tend to ramble when communicating to a group of people, you will need to address this opportunity. If you need development in this area, consider hiring a coach who can work with you on using effective communication skills to deliver the desired message. You might also consider joining a local Toastmasters Association.

Another uncomfortable issue in the work setting is that many women are perceived as people who can talk for hours about their kids and personal life, but struggle with holding their own in strategy sessions. If this analogy describes you, don't take offense. Recognize the perception for what it is, which is feedback. Spend your energy doing your homework on what relevant topics you can contribute at the next staff meeting. This effort will pay off in improving your self-confidence in arenas from which you typically shy away or avoid. A leader must have the ability to "hang with the power brokers" by demonstrating effective communication skills.

►People Development

People development leads to increased productivity, goal achievement, higher morale, increased commitment, and lower turnover. Therefore, effective leaders develop people. They help people grow personally and professionally. Sometimes these leaders are called mentors, sponsors, and coaches. The title isn't as important as what they do. Effective leaders take an interest in helping others become better. They set aside time to talk or meet with people they are developing. They help people work through the formal and informal culture of the organization. Sometimes people know their jobs and understand the organization's formal culture and yet are not successful. Why? Perhaps they don't know or understand the informal culture of the organization. They may not be familiar with the nuances of getting on the calendar of particular people with whom they need to meet. They may not realize the importance of using certain organization terminology. Leaders help bridge these gaps.

We remember having a boss who said, "whenever you go to repair a piece of equipment, be sure to take someone else to show them." We have expanded that statement to mean, whenever you are attending a learning session or situation, take someone else so that they are exposed to the information." If you are unable to take someone, then bring the information back and share it. This philosophy has served us well over the years. Ann understood that developing her people created more time for her to be the team's strategic leader.

Whenever you are in a position to influence people development with organizational resources, do it. People development, accompanied by an assessment, is a part of the culture in many successful organizations. It is an expression that the organization views its people as valuable and potential leaders. According to psychologists, few people ever use more than fifteen to twenty-five percent of their potential. As individuals increase their potential skills and abilities, we all win. One of the best opportunities is to talk development at specific times of the year—either as a part of the performance review cycle or as a part of a separate development discussion cycle. Our recommendation is a separate session that is totally focused on development with a written plan of action. Do it near the budget time so that the dollars are set aside for training and development. An effective leader can tell you the people they have helped develop over the years.

People development is helping people perform better at what they do and how they do it. It is also about helping develop people to assume positions of more responsibility. People development is one of those competencies you learn by just doing. The more you do it, the better you become. You know that you are doing well with people development when people are performing in their current position, when they are able to assume additional responsibilities, and when they are deemed promotable. Do what you can where you can. That includes helping with the development of people outside the formal corporate structure. This can be done through community, social, political, education, and religious organizations. Some organizations participate in mentoring programs where they mentor women from other member organizations.

Women in leadership roles must be prepared to give feedback that is appropriate for the situation. Too often they get caught up in the "desire to be liked" quagmire. If you need to reprimand someone, arm yourself with the facts, and give feedback as objectively as possible. Deliver the message in a professional manner. People will learn to appreciate your feedback as long as you give it with dignity and respect.

Regarding self-development, women must learn to be creative in getting the development they need. Too often others ignore their development as a way to hold women back. Therefore, take responsibility for your own development. If you have an area of weakness, you must take responsibility for correcting the area by seeking the necessary resources. Keep the mindset that you must always be in a learning mode. Volunteer for projects where you can learn something as well as utilize your strengths; just be sure the project is visible enough to warrant your efforts.

▪►Team Building

Leaders build high performing teams that are able to set goals aligned with their mission, develop a plan of action, and execute that plan. They are able to motivate themselves, hold each member accountable, set guidelines, and even develop a team culture. Every team must have a leader, and that leader ultimately has total accountability for the results. Effective leaders understand that every team experiences various stages before it is performing at a high level, and assists the team in successfully moving through these stages. The more effectively and efficiently the team is able to do this, the sooner they are performing at a high level. **The four stages in the development of a high performance team are:**

+ **Stage One:** The team should be formed with the team purpose in mind. Effective leaders base their selection of team members on the diversity of needed competencies and skills, and each team member's strengths. Leaders are open to new and different approaches and processes.

+ **Stage Two:** People may have differences of opinions about what to do, who should do it, and how it should be done. Make sure all team members have a clear understanding of the team's purpose. This is the stage when team members realize the size of the task ahead. This is also the stage where members have to deal with any issues they have relative to other team members, such as diversity of work style, communication style, gender, race, and many other diversity areas. An effective leader uses the opportunities this stage affords to encourage communication between group members and helps in the resolution of any team differences. An effective leader also uses this as a key opportunity to help team members understand the value of the differences or diversity within the team to achieve the goals.

✦ **Stage Three:** The team leader has provided information about the competencies and skills that each of the members brings. The group is more focused on the assignment. They have resolved most of the issues inherent within the diversity of the team. They have consciously decided to work together and are more comfortable with each other as team members. They have begun to self manage. Effective leaders know this is the time when new leaders begin to emerge within the team, and the team leader is not threatened.

✦ **Stage Four:** The team begins to perform at a high level. People know their roles and responsibilities and are communicating with each other. They are very focused on reaching their goals and following through on action steps, and they have developed a sense of trust within the group. Team members keep commitments and know that they can depend on each other.

As the team moves through the different developmental stages, the effective team leader makes the appropriate adjustments in their behavior to allow the team to develop to its fullest. The team leader should only be the enforcer if team members are not able to work together to resolve the issue.

A team that has evolved to high performance status, such as Ann's, requires that the leader is open to sharing some of the decision making power. An equitable way to accomplish this task is to identify team roles and expectations. When team members understand their role as well as the role of other members, the team can accomplish results faster. The opportunity for conflict is diminished because everyone understands his or her boundaries. Like Ann, you may understand the value of working through your people instead of you attempting to tell everyone what to do each day. If so, you are well on your way to being an effective team builder and leader.

A team leader establishes trust by honoring that when a team member makes a mistake, the discussion is held privately and centers on the individual learning how the behavior affected the team. Once that level of understanding is achieved, then the leader can let the member making the mistake determine how the issue will be communicated to the team. This action will go a long way in creating internal loyalty.

An effective team leader holds each member to the same standard of conduct. If commitments are made, they are to be honored. By being consistent in how you hold every team member accountable, you minimize opportunities for misunderstanding and hurt feelings. Like Ann has discovered, women who desire to be leaders must learn to strategically build teams that will support your leadership.

Your team can also be your peers. You will need people who are willing to share information. One way to build a sense of teamwork with your peers is to find out what their needs are and provide them with resources that will help them achieve their goals. A word of caution is required on this subject. Be cognizant of letting your desire to demonstrate teamwork become such a priority that you take on too many assignments because no one else wants to do it. People will dump on you if you allow them to do so. Think strategically. Volunteer for team roles that will also help you achieve your goals. This thought may sound selfish, but it's vital. Leaders must learn to discern activity from results in order to reach the level of respect that it takes to move up the organizational ladder.

Leveraging Diversity

Diversity means difference in every respect. Effective leaders know how to leverage diversity and they define it very broadly. They understand the importance of using diversity to achieve the best thinking and highest performance of people within their organization. Effective leaders embrace the importance of difference and support diversity with every possible opportunity. These leaders are aware of the ever-changing environment that influences their organization. They are knowledgeable about demographic trends that impact the marketing of their products, and the buying patterns of super heavy users of their product. Effective leaders foster an environment of respect and teamwork.

They have examined their own biases that might negatively impact the people within their organization. They talk openly about the importance of diversity in significantly impacting the bottom line. Effective leaders are very focused on identifying the best people for getting the job done. They are astute enough to realize that they need a balance of different skills and approaches on their team. Effective leaders identify what is missing from the team that will prevent the desired accomplishments. They are fair in the treatment and selection of people for different assignments. They respond immediately to any comments and issues that negatively impact people and the organizational environment in which they work.

You too can embrace and leverage diversity in your personal and professional lives just as effective leaders do by taking the time to examine your biases.

Ask yourself these questions:

- ☒ How do you feel about diversity and why do you feel that way?

- ☒ Are you uncomfortable working with people with visible disabilities? If so, why?

- ☒ Do you prefer to work with only certain racial or ethnic groups? If so, why?

- ☒ Why are most or all of the members of your team of a particular race, gender or ethnic group?

- ☒ Do you think that people of higher ranks in the organization are more intelligent than people at lower levels? If so, why?

- ☒ Do you think that women must play golf in order to get ahead? If so, why?

☒ During a business meeting, would you choose a male or female to go for coffee? Why?

☒ Are you uncomfortable working with people who are of a same sex orientation? If so, why?

☒ Are you uncomfortable having people on your team who disagree with your ideas and approaches?

☒ Are you uncomfortable working for someone who is much younger than you?

☒ When you hear someone with a dialect, do you immediately wonder how they could have made it to Executive Vice President of the organization?

These questions represent only a few areas where you may start to challenge your thoughts and behaviors in the leveraging diversity competency area. You might recall our discussion in Chapter Three where we talked about the impact of family, religion, education, race, and sex on our personal and professional lives. Many of our beliefs and related actions are based on our early life influences and may have no merit today. Challenge your biases, realizing they impact your perception, recognition, and treatment of people. Make the necessary changes.

Ann appreciates and supports diversity. She knows the value of leveraging difference. Her team of seven people is comprised of four females and three males. They are African-American, Latino, Asian, White, and Native American. There are age, experience, and cultural differences, as well as education and skill level differences within the team.

Consider learning more about other people, their cultures, conditions, and beliefs in order to understand and embrace diversity more fully. Spend some time getting outside your comfort box and get to know a different group of people. Read a different newspaper or magazine. Seek a different perspective on an issue. Rather than deciding someone cannot possibly be right, take the time and argue his or her position.

Too often women are limited to playing a specific role that may not allow for significant contribution because males dominate the team or committee. In the 21st century, the "good ole boy" network is still present. An example would be the lack of a significant number of women serving on the boards of major corporations. A woman's ability to think out of the box with workable solutions does not always receive the recognition deserved. Earlier we talked about the importance of staying in the fight. We all must continue to fight the gender gap to ensure that women who deserve to be in a leadership role are afforded the opportunity. Look for ways you can align with other women to encourage each other. Work towards doing more than having your name on the list of networking associations. Work hard to get involved and demonstrate leadership. As women, if you want things to change at the corporate board level, you must learn to mentor and nurture each other better.

Women cannot afford to believe that they have a better chance to be accepted due to their ethnic background or gender. This advantage is a myth. As competition becomes more and more aggressive, decision makers will be seeking leaders who can make an impact. Every now and then a token female may get a shot at the brass ring for appearance sake. This type of behavior is unacceptable. Women need to compete to ensure they are the best-prepared candidate for a position. Period. If not, and you are chosen for any other reason, don't be surprised if you are relegated to a non-power role.

According to research by Catalyst, in 1999, 11.2% of board members at the largest companies were women. In December of 2003, the number had grown to only 13.6%. What is it going to take for women to be placed on highly visible corporate boards? The answer—tenacity, know how, experience, connections, networking, and the support of other women and men to see as many women as possible move into leadership positions. If you align yourself with the type of people who are supportive of you and your goals, one day we will see the trend change to a significant number of women being in charge as the norm. Minority women need to ensure they are not left out of this vision by being open to others who don't look like them and learning from them. Build your network to include other diversity. Once you are accepted and on your way up the corporate ladder, reach back and help the next woman or women.

·►Leading Change

Organizations that want to be ahead of the curve and their competition lead change in their industry. The organization's mission, goals, product, customers, and the ever-changing environment dictate the appropriate change to make. Effective leaders lead change. They have a high level of awareness about current events, issues, and trends that impact their industry. They are knowledgeable about their organization and its goals. They are courageous and take calculated risks. They gather the necessary information and influence others to make the appropriate change. Leading change means being out front. It means taking responsibility for marching in a different direction. A change leader is an individual who has learned how to be flexible and adaptable so that the change does not create undo stress to themselves or others. A change leader does not mean that you become so flexible that you lose your identity and what you stand for. Follow your values. It does mean being open to the possibility of change as long as your values are not violated.

Effective leaders who lead change know there are usually three groups of people they need to identify. The first group of people quickly sees and understands the need to change, and they do. The second group of people eventually sees and understands the need to change but is reluctant because they have certain fears. After much coaxing and assurances, most in this group eventually change. The third group of people don't see or understand the need to change, and consequently don't.

You can be a change leader. Here are some ways to do it:

☒ Become more open to trying new and different approaches.

☒ Be unique and original in your thinking.

☒ Know as much as you can about the organization and industry in which you work.

☒ Stay current on events and changes that might impact your organization or industry.

☒ Determine changes that you want to influence based on the information that you have.

☒ Be bodacious and step up to the plate recommending a new procedure, benefit, product, process, or office location, and perhaps in some cases, no office at all.

Ann and her high performance team have recently developed a new process that positions her company far ahead of its competitors. Her ability to lead change has enabled her company to garner the market in her industry.

If you are yet uncomfortable about recommending major changes, you may want to start with small changes in either your personal or professional life. Then move to the changes that have a broader impact. Regardless of whether a small or large change occurs in your personal or professional life, make sure that you have done your homework and your recommendation for change has merit.

You can accomplish effective leadership through dedicated practice. Ann understood and focused on the five essential competencies for effective leadership each day. Her accomplishments did not go unnoticed. As a result, senior management now views Ann as a future senior executive. Like Ann, you can reach your desired level of advancement by focusing on developing your communication, people development, team building, leveraging diversity, and leading change competencies.

Chapter Five:

Words of Wisdom From Women Who Lead

W e identified and interviewed a very diverse group of twenty-seven female leaders who have made significant accomplishments in their careers. We used a combination of phone, mail, and in-person interviews. The guest contributor list includes women from different regions of the United States who are African-American, Asian, Caucasian, and Hispanic. We met our goal to include women who lead in a variety of career areas and who are at different levels within organizations. In each instance, we asked our contributors to provide tips and/or success stories on one or more of the five essential competencies necessary for effective leadership. The five essential competencies are:

- ☒ Team Building
- ☒ Leveraging Diversity
- ☒ Communication
- ☒ Leading Change
- ☒ People Development

We also asked them to provide tips or success stories on the overall topic of leadership.

These women were selected because of their significant leadership accomplishments in one of the following career areas:

- ☒ Academia/Education
- ☒ Community
- ☒ Business/Corporate
- ☒ Entrepreneurial
- ☒ Government/Politics
- ☒ Philanthropy
- ☒ Religion

Our contributors are excited about the opportunity to provide advice, tools, and strategies that could help other women in their quest to be effective leaders.

We have grouped the "words of wisdom" alphabetically by contributor and under the career category where the person plays a significant leadership role.

We are pleased to offer these words of wisdom from women who choose to lead and are very successful at leading.

Contributor's Response Chart

Category / Name	#	Page	Leadership	Leading Change	Communication	Leveraging Diversity	People Development	Team Building
Academia/Education	5							
Sarita Brown		58	X	X	X			X
Larine Cowan		59			X			X
Denise Hendricks		60	X		X	X	X	X
Dr. Linda Nicholson		61	X	X	X	X	X	X
Dr. Maria M. Vallejo		63	X	X		X	X	
Business/Corporate	7							
Anne Arvia		64	X	X	X	X	X	X
Jan Fields		66	X			X	X	
Patricia Harris		67			X	X		X
Cassie Nelson		68	X	X		X	X	X
Melody Spann-Cooper		70	X					X
Shawn Troy		72	X		X			
Janann Williams		73	X	X		X		X
Community	3							
Grace Chien		75	X	X	X	X	X	X
Michelle Porter-Norman		77	X	X	X	X	X	X
Anna Weselak		79			X		X	X
Entrepreneurial	5							
Georgia Dudley		80	X	X	X	X	X	X
Dr. Michele Hoskins		82	X	X	X	X	X	X
Cordia Wilkinson-Harrington		83	X	X	X	X		X
Dr. Cheryl B. Richardson		84	X			X		
Linda Vasquez		85	X	X	X	X	X	X
Government/Political	2							
Judge Willie Whiting		87	X					
Wyvetter Younge, Esq.		88	X		X		X	
Philanthropy	3							
Jackie Joyner-Kersee		89	X	X	X	X	X	X
Carmen Moody, Esq.		91	X			X	X	X
Anne Pettigrew		93	X	X	X	X	X	X
Religion	2							
Rev. Melbalenia Evans		94	X			X	X	
Rev. Dr. Emma Justice		95		X	X	X		
TOTALS	27		23	15	18	20	17	19

ACADEMIA/EDUCATION LEADERSHIP

From Sarita Brown

President
Excelencia in Education
Washington, D.C.

Sarita Brown worked with the Clinton administration as the Executive Director for the White House Initiative on Education Excellence for Hispanic Americans.

+ **Team Building:** Leaders are the catalyst. They need to have very good peripheral vision. Do the "walk around" to see what is going on and to stay in touch with your people. Remain open to what is going on around you. People are multidimensional, keep them engaged in terms of what they bring to the table.

+ **Communication:** Honesty, direct perspective, and a succinct message remains one of the most powerful ways to communicate. Communication is the catalyst for action.

+ **Leading Change:** Create an open channel between the head and the heart with your change message. Integrate the message with facts, figures, and emotion. I believe that people change because you give them better options. Bring problems with solutions to people who make the decisions about change. Change is the nature of life and the journey. It is not a choice.

From Larine Y. Cowan

Assistant Chancellor and Director
Office of Equal Opportunity and Access
University of Illinois
Champaign, IL

Larine is responsible for oversight of the development of affirmative action strategies, diversity education, outreach, and complaint resolution for some 10,000 employees.

+ **Leadership:** Early on, I understood three important principles of good leadership:
    1. There must be a willingness to continuously learn new things.
    2. You need to have a sense of humor.
    3. The art of getting things done lies in your ability to get along with other people.

+ **Team Building:** When building a team, my goal is to select the best and the brightest people who are capable of working together as a group in order to achieve the collective goals of the organization.

+ **Leveraging Diversity:** Ours is a rapidly growing world of diversity of people, cultures, languages, traditions, practices, values, and attitudes. Recognizing, understanding, and valuing this diversity in decision-making, service delivery, and marketing gives an organization a competitive advantage.

+ **Communication:** Sharing your thoughts, concepts, and feelings with others and getting them to understand is essential to moving your agenda through any organization.

From Denise Hendricks

Assistant Vice President of Human Resources
University of Illinois
Champaign, IL

Denise directs the human resources program for over 5,000 civil service employees. She also oversees academic appointment processing and benefits administration for the Urbana Champaign campus.

+ **Leadership:** It's more than taking a class. You learn from people you work for and with. Analyze what makes them successful. Observe other successful leaders and select the behaviors that best fit your style. I have adapted what I've seen other leaders doing.

+ **Team Building:** You build teams when people are working for the same goal. It is important that everyone understands how they fit in and how everything fits together. Team building is understanding, appreciating, and valuing what other team members do that supports the goals. An important step in team building is communication—sharing information throughout the team.

+ **Leveraging Diversity:** Organizations need people who bring different talents, knowledge, styles and thinking processes to the organization. Set diversity as a top priority. Train people on the importance of diversity within the organization.

+ **Communication:** Communication is a part of each of the other competencies. It should be frequent and channeled as deep as possible in the organization. People feel more secure when they have information. It is important to set aside time to have communication with your staff through staff meetings, one-on-one sessions, newsletters, e-mail groups, etc. Be a visible and accessible person.

✦ **Leading Change:** Change keeps everything interesting and challenging. Effective leaders see change as a necessity. They like and are enthusiastic about it. Change is a part of the world in which we live. One way to have your staff more receptive to change is to cross-train staff and periodically shift people around.

✦ **People Development:** Always look at your staff and be able to visualize potential beyond today. Have people work in collateral areas. Implement and use succession planning. Look for people who excel in one area, who might also excel in another. When people talk to you about their careers and development, take it seriously.

From Dr. Linda Nicholson

Professor and Director of Women and Gender Studies
Washington University in St. Louis
St. Louis, MO

Dr. Nicholson is the Susan E. and William P. Stiritz Distinguished Professor in Women's Studies and History.

✦ **Leadership:** Know your leadership style and the strengths and weaknesses that come with it. Be sensitive to how your style accomplishes something and how it can be a weakness if taken to the extreme. Recognize and accept that leadership doesn't come in one flavor. Leaders can be very effective using styles that are different from yours. A lot of women are really ambitious, but they have trouble using that word. They like power and the ability to effect change. I suggest getting comfortable with the word ambitious and going after the promotions to higher positions.

✦ **Team Building:** Remember that it is not just your ball of wax or your baby. There are people around who have a vested interest in the project as well as you. You don't have to solve every problem and then take it to others for validation. Work to get the appropriate groups/teams involved in solving issues and problems. They really are interested in helping with the resolution.

✦ **Leveraging Diversity:** Diverse groups of people don't just bring themselves. They also bring networks, communities, and resources. In academia, people know people; they talk about people and their achievements. This provides information on a larger pool from which to choose. When I teach a course on women's history and at least one person is African American, I look at history differently and see other perspectives. Inclusion—make this discussion a part of an entire history program.

✦ **Communication:** Sometimes women tend to shut themselves up too much. We don't give ourselves enough space to say dumb things and to make mistakes. We second guess ourselves and worry about what other people are going to say about us. Women don't want to be seen as greedy or aggressive so we ask for less. We usually bargain much less effectively than men. An example of this is in the area of salary negotiations. I recommend that you get as much information as possible. Arm yourselves with facts and figures. Know the average pay scale for the position. Practice saying to yourself, "I have great value." Ask for what you are worth.

✦ **Leading Change:** Create some strategies for leading the change. Look at what people have done. Talk to people who have done it in other places—don't reinvent the wheel every time. Find out how people are invited to conferences, publish articles, and get grants. Be conscious of whether you are whining or have some specific solutions for the problems that you see.

✦ **People Development:** Don't be shy about asking people to make contributions or go in another direction. Your request may stimulate their own creativity and can launch them into a new area of achievement. Share your ideas. Allow them enough room to be hesitant or say no. In the early 1970s

I was teaching in Albany, NY. I had been a feminist, but I had not yet made a connection between my politics and my academic work. I was asked to teach a course about politics and feminism. In the process of teaching this course, I ended up writing my first book.

There has to be an organization culture that rewards and promotes women. People have to be aware that the old ways are no longer acceptable. Women need to be an advocate of mentoring and collaboration.

From Dr. Maria M. Vallejo

Provost/Campus CEO
Palm Beach Community College
West Palm Beach, FL

Dr. Vallejo facilitates collaboration among diverse groups so that they may reach their full potential. She serves as a mentor and encourages her mentees to mentor others.

✦ **Leadership:** We have instituted an effective college-wide program called Leadership Enhancement and Advancement Program (L.E.A.P.) for women and minorities because we understand the importance of, and need for, having more prepared leaders. We also use the National Hispanic Leaders program as a resource for leadership development.

✦ **Leveraging Diversity:** Because we believe diversity is very important to our organization so we created a campus diversity committee to address this area as part of our strategic planning process.

✦ **People Development:** Every year I nominate a woman administrator to participate in the National Institute for Leadership. I am a board member and know the importance of all of us doing what we can to recognize potential leaders and to get them involved with ongoing programs and activities that help develop the necessary leadership competencies.

BUSINESS/CORPORATE LEADERSHIP

From Anne Arvia

CEO
ShoreBank
Chicago, IL

Anne is a respected corporate and community leader who has achieved a track record of pioneering in the banking industry.

+ **Leadership:** There is a difference in women leaders. We automatically bring diversity to the table when we choose to lead. Women should not feel the need to prove anything as you choose to demonstrate leadership, because all challenges can be managed. Credibility comes from having your hard work pay off. Our generation of women must decide to make a conscious choice to help other women excel. I believe the choice to lead happens at a relatively young age for most leaders as a part of their genetic makeup. You choose to be a leader in a certain area and you take action steps to dominate in the chosen area.

    My drive for leadership is to continuously be in a learning mode.

+ **Leveraging Diversity:** I view diversity broadly. It's not just about the number of minorities, their gender and race. People come from all walks of life; therefore, we bring different backgrounds and experiences. We must learn to recognize and be respectful of each other's differences. Leadership must start at the top in this area. Leaders must first conduct an internal inspection on how they broadly respect others and their differences. Be respectful and consistent in your approach to people. Your stakeholders look to you for direction in this area.

+ **Communication:** People learn in a number of different ways such as reading, listening, or actually doing. A leader needs to provide all forms of communication. Approach people in the way they are comfortable learning. Some people work best one on one. People are at different stages of development so if you have to repeat something ten times to help them, then understand, that's okay. Just ensure you are communicating in a manner that is comfortable for them.

+ **Leading Change:** I led a massive change process that shifted the entire culture of my organization. I didn't have all of the details when I initiated the change but I had the business case as to why the changes were necessary. Creating proactive change is the most important part of leadership. As a visionary leader it is important to always look for the next change that needs to happen and provide a clear explanation for why the change is necessary. People will still be scared about the changes but they will follow if you provide a vision that is strong enough and you are 100% committed to seeing the change take place.

+ **People Development:** People want consistency. They understand that as a leader you must provide direction. It is also important for them to understand that they are responsible for their careers. The leader's role is to provide the tools that give the individual the opportunity and skills to succeed. Be consistent in your message that everyone has an opportunity to succeed if they take responsibility for reaching their success. Always remember that non-performers affect high performers. The leader's role is to make tough decisions when people are not willing to perform after you have provided them the opportunity to succeed.

From Jan Fields

President, Central Division
McDonald's Corporation
Oak Brook, IL

Jan is responsible for the business results of 4500 restaurants in twenty three regions within a seven state geographic territory.

+ **Leadership:** Recognize that everyone looks to you as the leader so your behaviors are important. Realize that you set the example. If you want people to do the right thing, you must set the tone through your behaviors. People watch what you do to determine what is acceptable or not acceptable in the organization. Also, get rid of the ego. It's okay to let it be the other person's idea.

+ **Team Building:** It's important to have qualified people on your team that you have confidence in so you don't have to do it all as the leader. Be clear on your expectations and then allow people to do their job and contribute to the team results.

+ **Leveraging Diversity:** When I seek to add to my team, I don't look for people who look like me or think like me. I already have me. What I need are people who will oppose and challenge my viewpoint to ensure we get to the best viewpoint. I look for individuals who are experts on a particular subject and my role as the leader is to provide the balance.

+ **People Development:** People follow leaders they have confidence in and can relate to. Your credibility is tied to your ability to walk in the shoes of the people you lead and demonstrate how to add value through your actions.

From Pat Harris

Chief Diversity Officer
McDonald's Corporation
Oak Brook, IL

Pat Harris has won numerous awards for the leadership that she provides on many boards and with many business and community organizations.

✦ **Team Building:** As a leader your role is to create a positive environment that is supportive, communicates clarity of purpose and goals, embraces difference in its broadest sense, and recognizes and rewards contributions. The result is high performing teams where the productivity capacity of people is increased.

✦ **Leveraging Diversity:** The ability to influence and leverage the diversity of your organization is a key business imperative and critical competency for effective leadership. Make the time to understand the ever-changing faces of our diverse society and to create an environment where people feel included, appreciated, and valued.

✦ **Communication:** Providing clear, concise messages about the organization's values, beliefs, and expectations are a win-win for both the organization and it's employees. Listen better to communicate better.

From Cassie Nelson

Regional Vice President—Heartland Region
McDonald's Corporation
Kansas City, MO

Cassie manages a team that is responsible for over 700 restaurant units.

+ **Leadership:** True leaders lead by influencing others versus using any type of positional power. To motivate and inspire others to a point of getting them to do what you want them to and then having them believe and or feel that it was their idea is true leadership.

+ **Team Building:** Work hard at building an effective team. Select the best people and work with them to help them achieve their goals. When people believe that you are there to truly help them, they will go the extra mile to get the results. As a leader if you don't have the right players on the team, it doesn't matter what type of skills you have because the job/results won't be there.

+ **Leveraging Diversity:** When you accept/embrace your own differences as a valuable commodity; others will embrace them as well. I am a strong believer that we should all be able to be ourselves in the work environment. I qualify that by saying that you have to know the environment that you are in and understand how to make your differences work for you and create value for your team/company.

+ **Leading Change:** Change is inevitable. Change is good and we should embrace change personally. I believe that as an individual when you recognize the need to do things differently, learn more, and change the way you've always done things; you are more likely to accept, embrace and be an agent for change in your profession.

✦ **People Development:** People development doesn't always mean promoting people. It means telling the truth to the individual about their talents and potential. Coaching them and helping them develop a road map for success. It also means standing up for the people you believe in. I had bosses who didn't see the talent and potential of one of my managers. I worked with the manager to develop her. The bosses definitely see her talents today and support her continued growth with the company.

From Melody Spann-Cooper

President
Midway Broadcasting Corporation
WVON – AM Radio
Chicago, IL

Melody is a respected corporate leader in Chicago who uses her media expertise to provide leadership to the community.

+ **Leadership:** Any company's performance is a direct reflection of its leadership. Louis Carr, an Executive VP at Black Entertainment Television, once said, "In any organization, the leader is the visionary, and those who report to him or her are the paradigm builders." He helped me put my role and that of my team into perspective. I have to be an effective thinker and creator, and surround myself with responsible employees who can support and carry out my vision. Realizing that I too have weaknesses, it becomes imperative that I hire and surround myself with those individuals who are strong where I am professionally lacking, and respect and empower them so that the outcome helps the company win.

+ **Team Building:** It should be the goal of any successful leader to surround him/herself with nines and tens—employees who are on top of their game. However, there are some employees who fall short in certain areas, but have qualities that can benefit your organization. I think it is important to try to provide support for those who are lacking in some skill sets. Sending employees to workshops, or providing supporting material that can help them become better, speaks to your willingness to support growth. But if their individual performance is continuously affecting the team's collective efforts, you must cut your losses. Also it is important that you don't micro manage, especially when you have empowered individuals to take control over certain projects. Even as leaders, we can still learn. How empowering and rewarding it is for employees to have their ideas and concepts validated. To do so, builds loyalty and respect from those who work for you.

From Shawn Troy

I/T Specialist Team Lead and Project Manager
Organization IBM Business Continuity and Recovery Services
Chicago, IL

Shawn is an executive mid manager with IBM.

+ **Leadership:** I have learned during my many years in corporate America as well as in my personal life that the role of a leader is not "bestowed" upon you; rather, it is earned. The leadership roles I currently fill and the respect I have as a leader have been earned by exhibiting leadership behaviors such as valuing the importance of team building. I have executed my leadership roles by modeling the behavior of leaders I respect and admire. The behavior I always try to model is to "lead by example."

+ **Communication:** In my role as a Team Leader I attended a class in successful negotiations. Very shortly after completing this class I was engaged in a scenario that involved members of my team and another functional department in my organization. My newly acquired negotiation skills enabled me to conduct negotiations between these two groups, facilitating open communications regarding the issues of concern and not on the people involved. Over a short period of time we were able to create solutions to the problem in a manner that was mutually satisfying to both groups. Taking the self-development course helped me hone my communication skills.

From Janann Williams

Vice President of People
McLane Company
Dallas, TX

Janann Williams is Vice President of People for a nationwide logistics company supporting a staff of 15,000. She is known for her success in being able to link the People function to the overall organization business strategy, her ability to develop relationships, and her ability to build supportive teams.

✦ **Leadership:** As a leader, you cannot be just an observer. You are responsible for making things happen. Make decisions that cause people to move in certain directions. When you are a new leader in an organization, take the time to get to know the people and make it easy for them to get to know you. Ask questions and listen to the answers. If you want to make an impact, plan the process.

✦ **Team Building:** Create an environment for people to perform well. Act in a way that encourages people to feel connected. I do this by:

1. Taking the time to move around where my people work.

2. Asking them how they feel and what they think about what is going on.

3. Holding regular meetings with my staff so that they know what is going on, and so that

4. I know what is going on.

5. Having a team vision and goals.

6. Working on projects as a team.

Team building is a constant activity.

✦ **Leveraging Diversity:** As a leader, you have a responsibility to use diversity to grow the business. Diversity includes more than differences in race, gender, ability, and age. It also includes differences in philosophy, geography, education, competencies, thought processes, strengths, talents, and skills. Your job is to leverage those differences to get the team's best thinking and execution of the plan.

✦ **Leading Change:** I always ask, "Can we do it better, cheaper, or more efficiently?" Leadership and leading change are synonymous. Some change is easy and welcomed; some is not. You need to understand the culture and politics of the organization when you anticipate leading significant change.

COMMUNITY LEADERSHIP

From Grace Chien

Executive Director
Girl Scouts-Totem Council
Seattle, WA

Grace oversees an organization whose sole focus is on girls and creating opportunities and environments through which girls can develop to their highest potential. Based in northwest Washington, the organization serves 22,000 girls with a staff of nearly 100 employees in 8 locations and over 10,000 volunteers who reside throughout a 10 county region.

+ **Leadership:** Have the courage to say "I don't have all of the answers", and "I made a mistake". "Let's rethink my suggestion". Leaders make mistakes. Admit it, and move on from there. Your ability to do this encourages your staff to be willing to take risks and own up to their mistakes.

+ **Team Building:** We all depend on each other to get the work done. We (all staff) meet four times a year. The purpose of the gathering is in four areas:

  1. Increased communication,

  2. Better understanding and appreciation of each person and their responsibilities,

  3. Understanding our interdependence, and

  4. Professional development topics such as conflict management and resolution, communication styles, understanding and responding to people with disabilities, gender bias in predominantly female environments, and white privilege and institutional racism.

+ **Leveraging Diversity:** In the Girls Scouts we strive toward achieving a pluralistic organization. This means going beyond just being a diverse organization but instead an organization that values diversity in its systems and its culture. We work on engraining the value of pluralism throughout the organization and its functions, both internally and externally. This is critical for us because we are increasingly serving a larger and more diverse (religion, color, language, culture, etc) group of girls.

✦ **Communication:** Communicating effectively is always a challenge. It is even more of a challenge when your employees are in more than one location. Communication is important as a way to motivate and to keep staff focused on the vision, and in preventing and dispelling misconceptions.

✦ **Leading Change:** Lead change in the context of understanding the organization's core values. The process or product may change, but the values remain the same. Be open, candid, and willing to talk about the change that will be happening. Communicate information as soon as you have it. Ask for input from staff and where possible use it. If you are not able to use it, let them know why.

✦ **People Development:** Include in your annual budget a specific amount for each employee's training and development. Follow that with communication about the value of training and development, the availability of funds, and encouragement of employees to use the funds.

From Michelle Porter Norman

Zeta Phi Beta Sorority
Illinois State Director

As a State Director of an International organization, Michelle is responsible for coordinating the efforts of hundreds of women who provide needed community service.

✦ **Leadership:** Leadership is a <u>calling</u>, which only a few choose to answer. One is not born into leadership. It is a skill that has to be practiced over and over again. Your strength comes in the form of having the confidence in your own ability and the willingness to share in the leadership responsibility with so many others. Leadership should evolve, and with new leaders come new ideas, new vision, and new energy. The majority of people tend to follow leaders who are honest, visionary, inspiring, and competent. I try to display these components whenever a leadership opportunity presents itself.

✦ **Team Building:** As in card playing, you set your hand up first. The same holds true for team building. You set the right players in certain job responsibilities and trust they will give the task at hand the attention it requires. Over the years, I have discovered that when all parties involved understand that the ultimate goal is for the good of the organization or task, those who have the best interest of the group at heart will certainly rise to the occasion.

✦ **Leveraging Diversity:** I view the concept of leveraging diversity as two-fold:
    1. The way of making people feel as if they have a say in the decision making process by making the power base inclusive of all of its members, and
    2. It is the ability to relate to all different types of people, i.e. cultures, attitudes, religions, politics, age groups.

✦ **Communication:** Communication is the method of combining listening, talking, body language, and writing skills to get people to buy into the plan or goals. I use my strengths of motivating and achieving collaboration to attract those who are eager to a part of the goal setting process. Through various experiences, these skills have allowed me to either deal with matters in a favorable manner or have the courage to confront when necessary.

✦ **Leading Change:** I view change as a rebirth. Change is the belief that over the horizon something new and exciting is about to happen. The way a leader views change is the way change will be received by the membership.

✦ **People Development:** Through years of experience of dealing with all types of people I have learned that although it is more comfortable to try to please everyone, it is impossible. So rather than try, I ask myself in every developmental situation, "how would I want to be treated?"

From Anna Weselak

President
Oak Brook Area Association of Commerce and Industry--OBAACI
Oak Brook, IL

Anna is an entrepreneur and community leader. She also serves as president of the National Parent Teachers Association (PTA).

+ **Team Building:** Working as a member of a team is a win-win situation for me. Decisions made by teams are stronger decisions than those made by individuals. Participating on a team allows others to recognize your individual strengths.

+ **Communication:** The National PTA has taught me one of the best definitions for communication that I have found anywhere. Communication needs to be regular, two way, and meaningful. I have not yet found a situation where this definition does not apply.

+ **People Development:** In my business, I have learned that few people know their true potential. The more people can learn about themselves, the better they will understand others and the more productive they will be.

ENTREPRENEURIAL LEADERSHIP

From Georgia Dudley

President and CEO
Empowering Women Network, Inc. (EWN)
Chicago, IL

Georgia started EWN in June, 2002. Since then she has built an organization of over 200 members. The purpose of EWN is women helping women bring balance into their lives.

✦ **Leadership:** People follow those they can trust and depend on. A leader's actions must align with what she is asking of others. Leaders have followers. There are two types of individuals:

    1. Those who serve others and the world

    2. Those who take for themselves

Leaders are servants.

✦ **Team Building:** This is the most important part of the growth and strength of an organization. Understand the skill sets of your people and use them to the advantage of your organization. How can you help them build on the skill sets that they have? How can they be used in more than one capacity? Surround yourself with people who have the expertise and skill sets that are different than your own.

✦ **Leveraging Diversity:** Learn, listen and care about different cultures to better understand people.

✦ **Communication:** A vital part of communicating with others is the leaders own empathy, kindness and caring for others. There are always two sides of story. Embracing the fact that all of us are different and that our world is diverse increases a leader's ability to communicate with others.

✦ **Leading Change:** Always be moving forward! Ask yourself, are we moving? Be a visionary who is able to hear an idea and make a quick decision on what needs to happen to have that idea come to life. Know your team and be comfortable going back to them and asking, what next?

✦ **People Development:** People development takes time. A leader must be willing to put time into "her" resources. Helping that individual meet his or her career goals is the leader's job. Again, it goes back to serving. Indicators that development is needed are: 1) lack of results, 2) change in demeanor or decrease in productivity, and 3) change in spirit and motivation.

From Dr. Michele Hoskins

CEO
Michele Foods
Calumet City, IL
The 'Syrup Lady'

The company's products can be found in over 10,000 stores nationwide. Michele has been featured 3 times on the Oprah Winfrey Show and on all major news channels. Her book *Sweet Expectations* was released October, 2004.

✦ **Leadership:** Know your business. Establish your values and lead with them. Make a spiritual connection, take care of your health, develop yourself, be sincere, be the example, treat people with dignity and respect, let people know their value to you and the organization, write thank you notes, send birthday acknowledgements, say nice things to people, know when to follow, and understand and respect time.

✦ **Team Building:** You build teams when you provide an environment of support and openness, and where everyone knows a little about what everyone else does.

✦ **Leveraging Diversity:** Know what you need and look for the people with the experience and training to do it. Look for diversity of ideas and approaches, etc. to grow your business, whether the organization is large or small.

✦ **Communication:** This is one of the most important competencies. You must be able to communicate your expectations very clearly and succinctly. Paraphrase as necessary. Ask people to repeat the information back to you if you think there may be misunderstanding. Take the time to clarify.

✦ **Leading Change:** Look at change as an opportunity. Let your employees know that you think change is constant and important. Be open to and support new ideas, approaches, and processes.

✦ **People Development:** It takes time. You must be patient with people. Make people feel a part of the organization and that they have opportunities for future growth.

From Cordia Wilkinson Harrington

CEO
Bun Lady Transport
Nashville Bun Company
Tennessee Bun Company
Nashville, TN

The 'Bun Lady' and her team bakes and delivers buns and English muffins to five fortune 100 companies in 40 states east of the Rockies, Caribbean Islands, Venezuela and portions of Germany.

✦ **Leadership:** Servant leadership works best. Our job as leaders is to open doors and opportunities for our team to succeed.

✦ **Team Building:** Believe in the individual. Believe the best of each member of the team. Talk about their accomplishments and success to others.

✦ **Leveraging Diversity:** The best team is one whose team members have diverse backgrounds and perspectives. The best teams provide a business advantage.

✦ **Communication:** Open communication creates trust. Sharing financial results with the entire team allows everyone to see how they can and are making a difference.

✦ **Leading Change:** Change is inevitable in every company. Create a culture where change is embraced. Each day we will have problems to solve. Know they are coming. Accept flexibility and change as a part of your job as a leader.

From Dr. Cheryl B. Richardson

President
CBR Consulting, LLC
Aurora, IL

Dr. Cheryl Richardson is an entrepreneur, networker extraordinaire, and plays a key leadership role on several boards and committees.

+ **Leadership:** Leadership at its ultimate means "servant leadership" for me. I think that as a leader, one must model the behaviors you expect from others. My greatest successes have been derived from working with members of my work teams or networks who have achieved their career success and have contacted me to communicate there was a particular behavior they observed in me that contributed to their goal attainment. This type of affirmation is invaluable.

+ **Leveraging Diversity:** I have found that tapping into the experiences of others adds to the potent possibilities one can achieve in any situation. During my tenure in Asia Pacific, I had the opportunity to work with colleagues from a variety of cultures. They provided me insights that were so enriching as we formulated decisions that were significantly impactful to the people we served. The innovations and creativity that resulted from these collaborations have been lifelong learning's for me.

From Linda Vasquez

President
The Linda Vasquez Company
Chicago, IL

Linda is an experienced management consultant who specializes in facilitation and training in the areas of Total Quality Management, Diversity Development, and Career Development. She started her company in 1992 after twenty years with two major global corporations.

+ **Leadership:** The difference between managers and leaders is that managers coordinate and control what is already there. Leaders bring new concepts and ideas. Leaders are visionary. They are able to inspire and create enthusiasm around a goal, direction or idea. It is important to note, however, that both managers and leaders are equally important. One cannot exist without the success and accomplishments of the other.

+ **Team Building:** Many women and minorities are taught, by their parents and others, that we have to do it all and on our own. This handicaps us. It's important to learn to work in teams and to be able to collaborate on projects. Overall, women seem to be more willing to include others as team members and more comfortable allowing leaders to develop within the team.

+ **Leveraging Diversity:** The diversity of skills, languages, competencies, learning styles, gender, age, race, and ethnic group, etc. can be the competitive edge for a company or organization. When top management understand this and sets the example, the rest of the organization will follow.

+ **Communication:** This is the most important skill in the world—period. A leader must be in a mode of communicating constantly. Don't keep people in the dark. Create an atmosphere for team members to share and communicate. Listen to what those around you are saying. Communicate with clarity, accuracy, and honesty. Disregard what we are being taught by many leaders today about it being okay to miscommunicate and use doublespeak.

+ **Leading Change:** When people trust and believe in their leaders, they are more open to be part of the change. Create an environment of trust and openness in your organization.

+ **People Development:** It takes time to develop people. It's not that we can't find the money or don't know how. In this fast paced world, it's hard to justify the time to do it and do it at an outstanding level. Sometimes we even think it's easier to do the work or task ourselves rather than take the time to train others. My dad used to say to his bosses, "Train me and train me at an excellent level and I will not only do the job, I will produce better results than you have had before."

GOVERNMENT/POLITICAL LEADERSHIP

From Judge Willie Whiting

Circuit Court Judge of Cook County (Retired)
Chicago, IL

Judge Whiting was in the first group of magistrate judges in the Circuit Court system and went on to serve in numerous judgeship capacities for over 35 years.

+ **Leadership:** I often think back and wonder how my life would have been different if I had not fought so hard to resist others attempts to put me in my place. I now realize that the people that wouldn't help me were just thinking of themselves. They weren't necessarily trying to hold me back. However, because they wouldn't help me, it forced me to fight as though I was drowning in order to survive. As you work to establish your leadership role in life, fight as though your life depended upon it. If you are put upon unjustly, you know it, and so does the other person. If you have to fight back, do it in a civilized manner. Be fair to people. You will ultimately win in the long run.

From Wyvetter Younge, Esq.

State Representative
Springfield, IL

Illinois State Representative Younge, of the 114th district, has represented the interests of her constituents for more than three decades.

+ **Leadership:** Your focus needs to be on issues that affect your constituency. Make sure you are dealing with real problems, and not just cosmetic ones. It should be a community goal to train leaders for resurgence in the direction and in the agenda needed by urban areas.

+ **Communication:** Public service is about communication. You must listen to what is being said and what is not said. Understand the position from which the other person is coming. People want to know what is going on and what you are doing to represent them. That is true in any leadership arena.

+ **People Development:** Exposure develops people—exposure to new and different ways, approaches, information, theories, etc.

PHILANTHROPIC LEADERSHIP

From Jackie Joyner-Kersee

President and CEO
Jackie Joyner-Kersee Foundation
East St. Louis, IL

Jackie has built one of the most illustrious athletic careers in the world, earning the titles, "World's Greatest Female Athlete" and "Queen of Track and Field". She has netted 6 Olympic medals. Off the field, she has created the Jackie Joyner-Kersee Foundation and has built the Jackie Joyner-Kersee Community Center in her hometown of East St. Louis, IL

- ✦ **Leadership:** Find a way to inspire and move people to do something that they will continue to do without you always being there. Help people set realistic goals.

- ✦ **Team Building:** When you are the head coach, you have the responsibility to know the strengths and skills of all of the players. Add people to the team whose skills and strengths complement those of players already on the team.

- ✦ **Leveraging Diversity:** Diversity in your organization is a business advantage. It provides an opportunity to think outside the box—to experience new and different approaches. With the changing demographics of our nation, organizations need to be able to show that they have the work environment that can attract, support, leverage, and retain diversity of all kinds.

- ✦ **Communication:** Be able to talk with people who are at every level without losing site of who you are and what you want to communicate.

+ **Leading Change:** Be able to recognize the need to make a change before a situation escalates out of control. Be able to communicate the importance of change, knowing that everyone will not embrace it.

+ **People Development:** Know yourself well enough that you can help people see their weaknesses without realizing that you have helped them do it. Communicate with people in a way that lets them know that they are competent and capable of accepting new challenges and learning new skills.

From Carmen F. Moody, Esq.

Retired Attorney
West Palm Beach, FL

Carmen spends countless hours volunteering with local community organizations. She has always been drawn to those causes and situations where people, for various reasons, were unable to speak for or represent themselves.

✦ **Leadership:** We are often thrust into an unplanned position of leadership. In order to be more effective, I recommend starting early to prepare mentally, spiritually, emotionally, and physically for this role. Develop the skills of listening, communication, setting goals and execution.

✦ **Team Building:** When I led a very diverse team to raise over a quarter million dollars within six months for a community organization, our success was grounded in a collaborative effort and respect for the value that each team member brought. We met as a committee to: 1) brainstorm and discuss creative and innovative ideas to raise funds, 2) discuss and agree on a dollar goal, and 3) determine what was needed to reach the goal. Each team member volunteered for an area because of personal or professional strengths. As a key leader, I did whatever was necessary to support the team members. After reaching our goal we celebrated and thanked all of those who were an integral part of our success.

✦ **Leveraging Diversity:** When you live and work in an environment of diversity, you develop sensitivity to various styles of working and problem solving. At the firm, we built our law practice with diversity of all kinds: gender, ethnic, racial, philosophy, prior work experience, etc. This diverse work environment let our employees, our legal colleagues, and our clients know that diversity was a priority in our organization.

- **People Development:** This was a key role for me. I worked with new attorneys and support staff from day one. We were aware and supportive of employee development and made sure that it was aligned with employee needs and the firm's overall goals. An eager listening ear, daily encouragement, and formal and informal training must be a part of the development strategy for any organization.

From Anne Pettigrew

Philanthropist
Chicago, IL

Anne has worked tirelessly in the philanthropic area for many years. She is known for her dedication, ability to build teams, and fundraising.

+ **Leadership:** In leading, first and above all have integrity— keep your word. Be open-minded, resourceful, and diplomatic in resolving differences. Be a good listener. If you listen, you will learn what you don't know. Recognize people and what they do with a word, note, or call.

+ **Team Building:** As you work on forming a team, bring people from within and outside the group who have the best abilities. Ask them where their talents and skills fit and let them work with other team members to do the job. People on teams have to have a sense of pride and know what role they play in producing the end product.

+ **Leveraging Diversity:** You never know who will have the best ideas and contributions. Be open to and encouraging of the differences in people and how they think. These differences lead to best ideas and contributions.

+ **Communication:** Use any means of communication available to get the message to people. Communicate with respect. Believe in your cause, be upfront, and deliver your message using stories, preferably personal stories.

+ **Leading Change:** I think change can be hard to take. Recognize the need for change and its benefit to your overall organization. As leaders, if you are not really ready for the change, move on.

+ **People Development:** Let your people know that you believe in and have respect for them. Offer your services to be of help—have and use an open-door policy. Recognize people and their contributions at every opportunity.

RELIGIOUS LEADERSHIP

From Rev. Melbalenia D. Evans

Executive Minister
Trinity United Church of Christ
Chicago, IL

As Executive Minister, Rev. Evans plays a major leadership role in Trinity United Church of Christ. She is a second career clergy person who returned to school to achieve the academics necessary for her vocation. Trinity United Church of Christ has an active membership of 8,000 people.

+ **Leadership:** Women who aspire to become leaders should prepare themselves in four areas: 1) formally or academically, evidencing commitment and dedication, 2) informally by finding a mentor who is respected in the field of endeavor, 3) by creating a significant support group that will lend a listening ear, helps you with the other aspects of life impacted by your position, and they lend you their shoulder. My support group consists of friends who believe in the work that I do. They assist me in many ways including babysitting. They are the ones who allow me to unload emotional baggage. They provide a shoulder upon which to cry, and 4) finally, women of faith must be intentional in developing and nurturing a spiritual relationship. Your spiritual connection will aid you in times when it seems that all else has failed.

+ **People Development:** Mentors are those who are willing to assist you in decision making and who make time to guide those they are mentoring over the rough hurdles. I have enjoyed the privilege of being mentored by people of tremendous faith: The Rev. Dr. Jeremiah A. Wright, Jr., The Rev. Barbara J. Allen, and the Rev. Wendell Phillips. They have contributed immensely to my professional development.

From Rev. Dr. Emma Justes

Northern Baptist Theological Seminary
Lombard, IL

Dr. Justes is a Professor of Pastoral Care and Theology. She has mentored many ministers over the years.

+ **Leveraging Diversity:** I was the first woman minister to join the group when I took my Introduction to Pastoral Care courses years ago. In my initial meeting, one of my colleagues stated upon my entrance, "Now we have someone to fix the coffee." Over the years I have helped my colleague see how his viewpoint was incorrect that day as well as any other time, and we have become good friends. As a pioneer, I have learned that it is important for women to recognize what we are up against in order to create change for women within our culture. We must grow awareness about what we have to offer. Only then can we see the possibilities and have the courage to break out of a perceived role and go into new territories.

+ **Communication:** Human beings have the most trouble with being an effective communicator due to having no patience to listen to others. Women who desire to be effective leaders need to develop excellent listening skills. I view it as a gift from God to be able to have the patience to hear what other people are thinking. Think about how the rules will change in your families, communities, and in business if you only take the time to listen and learn.

+ **Leading Change:** In my research on women behaviors, I have found that women will fall into roles that men create, even when we know that role or definition doesn't fit us. I have watched women move into pioneering positions and behave as a man in order to be successful. They forget that the women's viewpoint is very much needed in this world. Before people change, they are in a state of unawareness. As you improve your awareness of what you offer, learn to be people of courage: Believe your feminine strength is the foundation to walk into any environment and create change that may be contrary to what our culture says it should be.

Chapter Six:

Lessons Learned - Narmen Hunter & Deborah Chima

O ur focus in this chapter is to provide you with some lessons learned from our perspectives. The process of learning these lessons falls into two categories: 1) comfortable, and 2) not so comfortable. Regardless of the category, they have helped us be better leaders.

Early on, we identified five essential competencies that are necessary for effective leadership:

1. Team Building

2. Leveraging Diversity

3. Communication

4. Leading Change

5. People Development

Our lessons learned are presented under these competency categories. In some instances, you may find that there is more than one lesson learned as a result of each of the experiences than we call out.

Lessons Learned—Narmen Hunter

My experiences have taught me many lessons. My goal in sharing these experiences with you is to provide some real events that have been milestones in my growth as a leader. Every situation is an opportunity from which to draw leadership lessons. What the lessons are depends on the situation, your attitude, your actions, and the results. These are some of my experiences and lessons learned.

Leadership

Situation: Balancing my professional and personal life has been a challenge for many years. I keep this challenge and how to meet it top of mind as my life continues to evolve. There is so much to do, so much to see, so much to enjoy, so much to impact, and so little time to do it.

The evolution to a more balanced life did not happen over night. It has happened over a period of years and as the result of several life changing events. A few of these events include college, marriage, mother, divorce, single mother, graduate school, corporate career, grandmother, and entrepreneurship.

In my early thirties I completed a program called "The Dynamics of Personal Leadership" by Paul J. Meyer of Success Motivation, Inc. (SMI). The company is now called Leadership Management, Inc. (LMI). The focus of the program is to help you better understand yourself—where you are now, where you want to be, and how to get there. I had to identify and write my strengths, opportunities (we called them weaknesses back then), values, and goals (with action plans) in six areas of my life:

1. Spiritual and Ethical

2. Family and Home

3. Mental and Educational

4. Physical and Health

5. Financial and Career

6. Social and Cultural

Everything seems to fall into one of these categories. This process had a major impact on my direction in life. The lesson learned is the significance of knowing myself and what is important to me as the foundation for determining what I do and how I do it. I still have tattered sheets with the goals that I have written over the years. I also have tattered sheets that show my accomplishments; I've reached most of those early goals.

There have been life cycles when I wasn't focused on balance, and I suffered the consequences. I stopped reading for months at a time. I didn't call my friends nearly enough. I didn't take enough vacations. I didn't smell enough roses. I didn't laugh enough, and I worked too hard and too many hours.

Making the time to learn more about me over the years helped me be more self-appreciative and enabled me to identify the kind of goals that are important in driving and supporting my life purpose.

People have played a major role in my success. They have inspired, excited, supported, and opened many doors for me. I am forever grateful. I have been blessed to be able to read people usually within a few minutes of meeting them. Consequently, I quickly know with whom I want to build lasting relationships—professional, personal, or a combination of the two. I also quickly know people who might present some obstacles along my journey. Other lesson learned: Identify the people, things, and things that have a positive influence on you and spend most of your time there. Let go of the things, routines, places, and people that negatively impact you.

One of the lessons learned that is most important to me is knowing when and how to say "no" and being comfortable after having said it. It took me a while to get there, but, oh, does it feel good to be able to say it now!

Action: I play many roles—mother, grandmother, sister, aunt, cousin, friend, mentor, neighbor, informed citizen, organization member, entrepreneur, and president of a small company. The balancing act is critical to my success in business and in my personal life. I take time to continue to know myself. I know the following about myself:

1. I am a very spiritual person.

2. My family is very significant in my life.

3. My grandmother played an important positive role in my life. How I treat and interact with my grandchildren is influenced by the way my grandmother treated and interacted with me.

4. My most productive thinking and creative time is in the morning.

5. I should not start to read email messages before 2:00pm.

6. I need to be in bed by 10:30pm.

7. I thrive on sunshine, flowers, beauty, laughter, music, and interacting with children.

8. I need to make a contribution that makes the world better as a result of my being here.

9. I love photography.

10. I tend to surround myself with people who are optimistic, spiritual, fun loving, and who are successful.

11. There are times when I need down time to do nothing—absolutely nothing.

Result: I have achieved 90-95% of my early goals and continue to achieve the goals that I set. One of my career goals in 2004 was to increase my client base in three specific regions of the country. That has happened. I continue to set annual goals and make an annual plan that includes my top priorities—time with my grandchildren and other family members, vacation time for me, client assignment time, and client building time.

My grandchildren live in another state, and I am able to visit with them at least monthly and sometimes twice a month. I currently mentor five young women and stay in contact with most of those I have mentored over the years. I take more time to relax with less on my list to do. I am reading more and snapping more pictures.

The more I stay focused on the six life areas and the priorities within them, the better I am able to balance both my personal and professional life. Most of the time it works. When it doesn't, I remind myself that tomorrow is another day.

►Team Building

Situation: As the department head, of a fortune 100 corporation, I led a team of people who decided that we wanted to win a national award in our discipline. I knew that we had the team players who could make it happen, so I approached the team about going for the award. It would be the first time our regional human resources department had won this award. The major lesson learned is that clarity of purpose and goals, focus on the action plan to reach the goals, and a reward that is valued by all team members are keys to success. A second lesson learned is the value of having the interest and support of your supervisor in a major effort.

Action: In our first meeting, I talked about the requirements, the hard work, and the rewards for winning. Winning would bring the department and its staff, a much higher level of respect within our region and throughout the system. Winning also carried with it a substantial cash award for each member of the team. Even in the preliminary discussions there was so much excitement. Our team's performance and strong results were already known throughout the region and in several pockets of the larger organization. But it was not enough to win the coveted award. We knew it would take a great deal more. We also knew the importance of working together in reaching the goals. We met as a team to discuss our department goals for the upcoming year and the strategies for reaching them. We wrote specific and realistic goals. We knew that in order to win the award we needed to stretch. We also knew that achieving and receiving the reward would be worth all of the work. We were very clear about what needed to be done, who would do it, and how it would be done.

I advised my boss that the human resources department was going for the national award. He was very supportive. On a monthly basis, I reviewed our results against the goals with the team and with my boss. We stayed focused on the action plans. We charted and tracked everything related to the action plans. We talked about what we were doing and what was working. We also talked about what wasn't working that we probably needed to change. My boss continued to be very supportive. Communication was an integral part of our strategy. We had to know at all times, where we stood. I made myself available to the team for any questions or needed resources. It took all of the team members pulling together to make it happen. Each of us felt we had a responsibility to do our part.

Result: The department reached its goal of winning the national award. We received the cash reward, and we celebrated. Even years later as I write this I feel the excitement of those days and I smile at the sweet taste of victory. The process of working to win the award made us a stronger team, produced a closer working relationship, and brought a level of excitement and focus that had been missing. The respect for the department soared even higher. Suddenly we were known throughout the system of this fortune 100 company. Team members felt more confident as we approached our annual planning for the next year. We knew what we were capable of as a team. The result of our effort was a positive impact on the region's bottom line. We felt like a profit center rather than a cost center.

▪️▶️Leveraging Diversity

Situation: I was a part of a voluntary team of women who came to-gether on an annual basis to raise funds for a local charitable organization. The membership included women of different race and ethnic groups, and religious denominations. It also included women from various companies, organizations, occupations, and positions. Some of the women were depart-ment heads and managers, while others were students. Some of the women had board and voluntary experience, and a few did not. Most were working, and a few were retired or moms-at-home. Three or four were long-time volunteers. The ages ranged from early 20's to mid 60's. Some of the leadership positions of the group changed on a regular basis to give those interested an opportunity to serve in various leadership capacities. Members of the team used their differ-ent expertise, knowledge, positions, passions and contacts to raise thousands of dollars each year. I chaired one of the sub-committees. An important lesson learned is that each person brings their own resources and contacts which increases the audiences receiving your message.

Action: After each annual luncheon and fashion show we decided on the chairperson and the dollar goal for the next year. We normally had two volunteer co-chairs to lead the team. Members either volunteered or were asked to serve on vari-ous subcommittees. Subcommittee chairs volunteered, were assigned, or were recruited. Most volunteered. The co-chairs leveraged the diversity of the full team.

As the chair of the Publicity/PR subcommittee, my role was to leverage the diversity of our subcommittee to get the word out, as far and wide as possible, about the annual gala., thus increasing ticket sales. Given the busy schedules of the subcommittee members, we used telephone conference calls as the primary mode of communication. As a first step, I talked with each of the subcommittee members about their expertise, contacts, and responsibility preference. As a second step, and as a group, we decided on the people, places, and publicity methods to be used. We had an artist-type in the group, so she was responsible for the design and printing of the posters that advertised the gala. She used her skill and contacts to get that done. Another member of the Publicity subcommittee knew someone who owned a PR firm and who could provide us with contact names, addresses and numbers. Another member of the team had contacts in an area where we had tried to advertise but without much success.

Each subcommittee member brought their own group of contacts and resources. I developed a short survey that we asked each guest at the gala to complete. We used the information received from the survey to determine where people were getting information about the annual gala, and as a guide on where to advertise. We also leveraged the diversity of each team member. I asked them to provide contact names and resources. They did.

Result: By leveraging the diversity of the Publicity/PR subcommittee I was able to get information about the annual benefit gala to a much larger audience, using several different venues. We were successful in raising thousands of dollars for the local charity.

Communication

There have been several instances where I thought I had communicated a message clearly or understood a message someone was communicating to me only to learn that what I thought I heard was not said. In some instances, what I thought I said was not heard. Communication is about more than just saying words. It's about clearly expressing thoughts, listening, clarifying when appropriate, paraphrasing and asking questions—the right questions.

Situation: I was meeting with Bill and James to review a project. Bill mentioned the name of a colleague we both knew—Ron Brown, saying that Ron had just died. Bill went on to express his sorrow. Since Ron Brown had served as a consultant to me and others in my company, I said that I would pass the message about his death to those who had known and worked with him.

Action: Before I left to advise others, Bill sought to get clarity on the matter, probably wondering how I knew Ron Brown (former Secretary of the Interior). As a result of Bill digging deeper, we learned that he and I were speaking of two different people with the same name. The person I was speaking about was an external consultant who had the same name as a very prominent national political figure who had just died.

Result: I learned the correct information in enough time that I did not pass erroneous information to others. My credibility within the organization could have been seriously damaged, not to mention the emotional impact of the erroneous information on people who knew the consultant. It was a wake up call to me, an important lesson learned, about the importance, in every day conversation to seek clarity and understanding. Listen, ask questions, paraphrase, and provide relevant information.

►Leading Change

Situation: I was a part of a large organization that did not have standards in place for measuring success with some of its key customers—our employees. I was also a part of a three-person informal networking group within the same organization, that often discussed human resources issues and possible solutions. Important lessons learned were: Informal groups with a purpose and focus can have a major impact on an organization. It is important to know and understand an organization's structure and culture when anticipating leading major changes within that organization. You must be willing to take all of the necessary steps to lead, influence, and implement change. Understand the roles different people play in assisting with the change effort. Change does not occur overnight. It is a process that takes time.

Action: As a first step, we talked with the executive officer who sponsored the team. She agreed about the need for people standards, supported the idea of getting standards adopted throughout the organization, and knew we needed to get the larger team on board for this to happen. Together our three person informal group brought this to the larger team as an agenda item. Our goal was to get the team to understand the need and business value for people standards. After a few meetings and lots of talking, the larger team decided that we should move forward with the work on people standards. The next step was getting the larger team to champion standards throughout the organization.

The team leader talked with people at her level and above. Members of our larger team started working within their divisions and regional areas. Again, they did a lot of communicating and partnering with the departments and units directly affected. The field teams got involved. Each division, along with their regions, developed people standards based on their division, region, and unit's culture and needs. In the end, we developed a set of universal people standards, regardless of the division, region, or unit. In addition, people standards were developed that were more division and regional specific. With the help of many people, and over a 12-24 month period, standards were put in place within the company.

This change started with an idea based on my knowledge about the company and its culture, operations, and opportunities for the organization to treat its employees and customers better.

Result: The adoption of standards led to a significant emphasis being placed on the area of people (internal and external). The benefit of the focus was increased retention, lowered turnover, increased top line sales, and higher bottom line profitability.

►People Development:

Situation: I once had a boss who constantly said, "When you go to check or repair a piece of equipment, always take someone with you to train them. Use every opportunity to train and develop someone else." He was right. I was managing about 60 people in an environment where turnover, because of promotion, transfer, and termination, could happen at any time and did significantly impact operations. Important lessons learned were: When people are provided the opportunity, training, and recognition they normally perform well. Timely and relevant training and development of employees helps employees, supervisors, and managers do their jobs better. Cross-training helps to build effective teams.

Action: People development on an ongoing basis was the saving factor. I selected a person to oversee the training function—scheduling the training time, scheduling a trainer, and following up to determine if the training was completed. The skills learned were charted next to the employee's name on a large board that was visible to all employees. Realizing that some of my employees could handle responsibilities beyond those normally accorded to their title, I started early preparing them for the next level. My focus was on developing people based on their ability and less on their position. People were excited about learning as much as possible and assuming responsibility of new and different areas of the operation. My assistants realized that the more they trained and developed people reporting to them, the easier the assistant's job was. We spent a lot of time cross-training employees. As a result, shifts ran smoother because people were able to help other employees as needed. When someone was not able to get to work for one reason or another, we had back up from the employees who knew their job, as well as, that of the person unable to come to work.

Result: Training was a part of the day-to-day operation of the business. We recognized and rewarded people who learned new stations. People were proud of their new skill levels. They met the challenges of the new assignment and performed their current jobs at a higher level. People were also less threatened by the responsibilities at the next level because they were more prepared for the position, and consequently more open to promotional opportunities. Sales increased, waste decreased, retention increased, turnover decreased, and profitability increased.

Lessons Learned—Deborah Chima

Learning to be an effective leader will encourage you to have confidence in your abilities. You have value to share. Every situation you have experienced is an opportunity from which to draw leadership lessons. I'd like to take this time to share some of my most valuable leadership lessons with you.

➤Leadership

Situation: I had a very successful career as a corporate manager. I received a promotion on an average of every two years. I was able to reach my career goals by being focused and driven. I had a track record of being able to achieve results in both the international and domestic markets to which I was assigned. I had no problem relocating if the moves led to a better position. To some of you, this scenario sounds like a dream come true. Yet there was a missing element. I was so focused on getting to the next position that I allowed my professional life to also become my personal life.

Action: Four years ago, during a time that I had a ground breaking international assignment living and working in the Caribbean, I reached a turning point in my life. A family crisis caused me to walk away from a great job without hesitation to return home. I had no job leads at the time and for a consummate workaholic, taking quality time off to care for my sick mother was the best thing that could have happened to me. That experience was the starting point that helped me to put my priorities in perspective. I eventually returned to work and would like to tell you that I was cured of having non balance. The truth is that I jumped right into some of the same behaviors in my attempt to prove my ability to lead in a new work environment. I did a little better with achieving more balance since my family was now in close proximity. Yet, work continued to be the priority. In retrospect, I had to experience burnout with the hustle and bustle of making things happen before I truly realized the toll this type of lifestyle was having on me physically.

Result: A valuable leadership lesson I have learned is to recognize the importance of creating separation between my personal and professional life. When I showed up to work sick, it sent the wrong message to my team. My behavior demonstrated that I did not value myself and it implied that I expected them to emulate me. What was I thinking? In retrospect, I was simply acting out my perceived role of a strong woman who had important responsibilities. I thought the organization could not function correctly without me. I poured my heart and soul into my work. While the organization benefited, I shortchanged myself by not having balance.

Launching a new business is very time consuming. I am learning to stop and smell the roses more often. This is not easy to do on a limited budget, but it's necessary in order to be at my best when I am at work. I am finding that when I clearly make room for down time with family and friends, or just doing nothing, I am much more energetic and focused about meeting my goals when I return to my work. In fact, my mind is now more open to trying new things, such as writing. I now realize that the ability to write was within me all the time. It took a bold move of dramatically changing my perspective of the importance of work in order to allow my other talents to surface.

Work is obviously still a priority, but now it has taken its rightful place in my life. I have had more vacations and just plain old down time in the last two years, since I left Corporate America, than I did my entire career. I have to admit that all along I was receiving signals that I was out of balance. I ignored the signals in the name of having a great career. I accomplished my career goals and thought that was enough to make me happy. It wasn't.

At the end of my corporate career, I was offered another opportunity to relocate. What sounded like a great offer to some, given my new mindset, was a possible death sentence for me. I had finally reached the point that the sacrifice of having to start over again in so many ways was no longer worth the price of being on a stellar career path. The best thing for me to do was to walk away. Amazingly, the organization didn't fall apart due to my decision. Funny how that played out, despite convincing myself that I was indispensable all those years. I don't advocate this type of life changing decision for everyone. I encourage my coaching clients to ensure they focus on having balance in their personal and professional lives long before burnout and disillusionment occurs. I encourage them to explore the talents and gifts that lay dormant waiting to be released. More important, I encourage them to take the time to have fun during their career journey so these talents can surface.

► Team Building

Situation: Sharing my private thoughts and mistakes with others in a work setting is an area from which I have previously shied away. My fear of rejection and the conflicting need to seek validation from others created internal barriers that prevented me from allowing others to get too close. In reality, during my years as a corporate manager, my focus on masking my fears sometimes came across as being a know-it-all. This perception created lost opportunities to build effective relationships

Leading others effectively means establishing trust. Trust was not an area I willingly explored as a corporate manager. My mindset was to get the job done without allowing the people who reported to me or my peers to get too close. Although I had a successful career, I now realize I limited myself by holding on to this type of thinking.

Creating a start up firm involves using as many resources as possible. The importance of interacting with people to determine their needs and how I can assist them has taken on new meaning as an entrepreneur. During the initial phase of my transition, I soon realized I had to change my thought process if I sincerely desired to be a leadership resource.

Action: I must admit that one of my mentors, Jylla Moore Foster, author of *Due North! Strengthen Your Leadership Assets*, helped me to accurately identify where I needed to start. Trust became the operative word. She effectively coached me on realizing that I was the barrier to establishing better work relationships. The first step was to acknowledge my fears in order to overcome them. The next step was to learn to trust my inner instincts to allow discernment to determine when it is appropriate to open up.

Learning to trust myself and my sincere desire to want to help others reach their goals helped me to overcome my fears. As a result of the coaching I received, I am now open to developing trust opportunities as I establish networks and teams that involve working with others. To be an effective member of the team, I have learned that it's okay to reveal your weaknesses as you build trust. Your gut instinct will guide you as to how much about yourself you should reveal in each situation.

Result: Sharing my life experiences has created client opportunities to demonstrate leadership. I am now open to sharing my weaknesses as well as strengths. Prior to my life changing coaching session, I would never openly discuss my weaknesses in a work setting. One of my most important lessons learned was to realize that others can benefit and thus receive value from sharing my ability to overcome obstacles despite the odds and self-inflicted mistakes. My clients have provided feedback on how they relate to my examples and thus learn from the discussions. I now sometimes wonder how much further I could have led my corporate teams if I had learned this lesson sooner. I now coach corporate professionals who desire to be more effective on the importance of establishing trust as they work to create high performance teams.

▶Leveraging Diversity

Situation: I love to use my leadership skills within the professional associations to which I belong. Inevitably, I am either elected or appointed to a leadership role. Normally, this sounds like a good match for a person who thrives on helping projects move forward. However, I would sometimes find myself in conflict with others on the committee that either had a different type of work background or set of values on how things should be done.

Action: In these types of scenarios I work very hard to understand the other person's perspective and where possible, I seek compromises that allow all points of view to be considered. This statement sounds simple but is actually very hard to do for someone who has a dominant type of leadership style. I have had to learn to improve my listening skills. By taking the time to really listen to the other person's perspective, I can ensure I understand where they are coming from before I begin to influence them on my way of thinking. I ask a lot of questions in my attempt to understand their position and I seek confirmation to ensure I have the right understanding. If people believe they have been heard, they become more open to hearing your perspective. It is only then that you will be able to help the group reach a compromise that is acceptable to all.

Result: I have learned to believe that everyone has something to contribute to the process due to their life experiences and backgrounds. I have had to learn and value that not everyone within the community groups to which I belong has the same mindset and sense of urgency to create and execute a plan. I have had exposure to many different cultures and ways of doing things through my work and community associations. Strong leaders often use their energy ensuring that they are involved in making every decision. I now better understand that it is the leader's ultimate role to spend more time providing an opportunity for every voice to be heard. The impact of many is always much greater than the impact of one person. Let everyone's opinion count by listening and clarifying your understanding of what they have to say. The end result will usually be a better product, service project, or team contribution.

Communication

Situation: As an African American female trying to survive the competitive world of Corporate America, there was always someone who wanted to challenge my authority or knowledge. Despite my high performing, documented results, at times I felt condemned no matter how hard I tried. Hurt by the perceived rejection, I could always rationalize why it was okay to communicate from my emotions rather than from my brain. The short term satisfaction that I would receive from verbally putting someone who unfairly challenged me in their place was usually short lived. I always experienced repercussions to my decisions to "let it all hang out" in my communication. When these career repercussions happened, I would continue to rationalize my emotional outbursts as justification for me not being treated fairly.

Action: I received feedback from a human resource professional, Robert Scharringhausen, whom I highly regarded, in language that helped me understand how my justification was actually hurting me. He helped me to see that every time I would allow myself the pleasure of an emotional outburst, I created a barrier with the person with whom I was interacting. Whenever an opportunity came up to verbally lambaste someone for a perceived slight, I would think about what Robert taught me regarding the importance of creating good working relationships. I learned to weigh the value of establishing a potentially great partnership against the short term satisfaction of letting the person know how I really felt about their behavior.

Result: My lesson learned is that no matter how much individual satisfaction I received from saying exactly what was on my mind, I hurt myself in the long run in the area of building relationships. I have learned that when in a leadership role, you must be prepared for others to challenge or criticize you. If your motives are honest and your behaviors are consistent, you don't need to be so concerned with feedback from people who are clearly not in your support camp. On the days when you don't receive positive feedback despite giving your all, allow yourself to reflect on your accomplishments, and learn to praise yourself. People who are not in your corner will wonder how you can bounce back so easily. The real secret to ensuring your communication style is always professional is to keep them guessing on what motivates you.

As a result of taking Robert's advice, I worked hard to control my emotions when I felt I was being disrespected concerning my abilities. Therefore, I was able to build some great relationships in my organization, which I still have. My willingness to acknowledge and change my behavior resulted in becoming a more effective communicator. When I had a misunderstanding with someone at work, I would request that we meet one on one, and I would calmly let them know how their behavior negatively affected me. I would then let them know my preference as to how they should communicate with me in the future if they had an issue with me in any way.

I wish I could say that misunderstandings no longer occurred at work as a result of my changed behaviors. I can say that people challenging my knowledge or authority no longer caused me to react emotionally. I demonstrated my skills to my detractors by continuing to perform at a high level. I didn't let their negative communication cause me to get off track from reaching my goals. More important, I didn't give them more ammunition to use against me by communicating in an unprofessional manner. Another lesson learned—Let the focus be on what you accomplish, not on what you said to someone in the heat of the moment when being challenged.

·▶Leading Change

Situation: Creating the desired result of a project or task involves flexibility. In many leadership positions, I have constantly needed
reminding that to be flexible means being open to change
occurring at any time. I typically work best in environments
where expectations are clear and a foundation can be laid
based on the expectations. In one particular situation, I was
assigned to a corporate international team that involved
creating a new infrastructure for the entire organization.
Change on this team was constant and became the mantra of
the day because no one had ever gone down this path before
of creating a new operating system. Within a week of being
assigned, I realized that change for the sake of change was
getting us nowhere. Everyone on the team appeared to accept that the constant changes would eventually lead us to
greatness. Given my newfound desire to create better work
relationships, I was initially reluctant to speak up about the
impact all of the changes were causing on our team's overall
performance. We were busy but we weren't getting tangible
results. Would I be so bold as to let all of these high level
professionals know that from my perspective, we were just
going in circles?

Action: Given the diversity of the team and the cultural differences that
were at play, I strategically met one on one with the key team
members to gain an understanding from their perspective on
how the constant changes were affecting them. I discovered
that they were just as frustrated as I was with the stop and
start again process cycle in which we found ourselves. We
didn't feel empowered to create the environment that would
minimize or stop all of the unnecessary changes. We agreed
to speak up to the team leader to express our concern with
all of the activity, yet lack of results. In my bold manner, I
volunteered my thoughts whenever possible during the meeting, despite being the newest team member.

Result: The team leader was the type of director who was willing to let the team members determine our next steps as long as the steps lead to accomplishing our goals. As a result, Jean Louis turned out to be one of my better bosses. He encouraged me to speak up more often if I did not agree with our direction, in order to create the change in behaviors I desired. In all of my years of working, I had seldom been afforded that type of empowerment. He clearly believed in my abilities to get results. Giving me that type of freedom created a strong motivation for me to help him and the team succeed. I agreed to turn my life upside down one more time and live and work out of Canada to help the project succeed.

The lesson learned is that having the courage to go against the grain created an opportunity for me to demonstrate change leadership as well as assist the team with reaching better clarity on our goals. I now better understood how I could contribute to our success. Going out on a limb and speaking up created a better work environment for everyone. As a result, we became a more effective team and began to achieve and celebrate success. I am extremely happy that my last corporate position led to me finding my place on a team where my management style of being a vocal leader when things aren't going right, was accepted and embraced without others being threatened.

►People Development

Situation: While leading a previously non-performing team, I had to have some very tough and uncomfortable conversations with my team regarding their levels of performance immediately upon my assignment as the department manager. I had been a manager long enough to know that one of my immediate steps was to assess the performance of my supervisors. If they weren't effective, I would have a hard time getting the rest of my staff to perform at an outstanding level. Performance at any other level was not acceptable to me as I took on the challenge of turning the department's results around.

Action: I gathered my facts concerning the reasons for the non-performance and set up individual meetings. The initial meetings were used to establish expectations from both perspectives. I gave them an opportunity to communicate why they were currently delivering negative results and what they were going to do to correct the situation. I used my communication skills of being direct and specific to help the non-performers understand why their current results were not acceptable. I used my team building skills to paint the picture of where the team was headed and what role I needed them to play in our future success. Given the pressure to perform that I was receiving, the luxury of gradually making the agreed upon changes was not an option. I made sure the non-performers understood the time frame they had to work within to turn the results around.

I had to make the tough choice of either accepting non performance because it was the best way to get my new team to like me and hope that things would work out, or communicate how to achieve the results, hold them accountable, and realize that I was not always going to be popular. During some of my initial meetings it became clear that I was not going to be able to establish the desired partnership with some of the supervisors. We either had a difference of opinion on how realistic my expectations were or encountered a barrier due to my direct communication style. I implemented a development day process with each supervisor during which they had my undivided attention within their assigned work units. Some of the supervisors used this opportunity to honestly share some of their issues and we worked together to solve them. I began to notice the non performers were not comfortable with having so much direct contact with me because I could now observe their deficiencies up close, and those development days were not as productive. You can lead a horse to water but you can't make them drink.

Result: Within six months, our financial results trended positive, and within a year we exceeded the previous year's results by a large percentage. Once the team experienced the accolades and recognition that came with success, they were hungry for more. Adhering to high standards and not accepting excuses were the catalysts to turning our results around. The lesson is that as a leader, I had to become comfortable with making the tough call to allow non-performers an opportunity to improve their results and terminating them if they were not willing or couldn't make the necessary changes in their behaviors. Some of the supervisors I terminated were very popular even though they were non-performers, so I took some heat from my peers, their subordinates, and others, as a result of my decisions. I was okay with not being popular because I knew in my heart I had given these individuals more than enough opportunities to turn things around.

The supervisors who were marginal performers were given even more time because at least they were trying to meet the expectations. I worked with people on their development opportunities if they were willing to put forth the effort. During my tenure in this department, no one had any questions about where they stood in regard to performance and the amount of time they had to reverse the results. Leaders must communicate their expectations and hold people accountable. I am pleased to say that the high performers simply achieved even better results under my leadership style of being direct, focused, and results oriented. I am still in touch with them today, as I take pride in their continued accomplishments.

Chapter Seven:

Leadership Interactive Exercises - Making It Work For You

The purpose of this chapter is to assist you in the transfer of the knowledge that you have gained. This is an opportunity to apply the advice, tools, and strategies we have presented in the book to situations that replicate what is happening in many of your professional and personal lives. Application of the tools and strategies speeds the process of you choosing to lead, and your journey to being a more effective leader.

There are two exercises for leadership as well as two exercises for each of the five essential competencies:

1. Team Building

2. Leveraging Diversity

3. Communication

4. Leading Change

5. People Development

One exercise deals with Ann and Alicia, and the other asks you to decide how you would respond in a given situation. We recommend that you start with the exercise category that best fits your current environment. This helps you develop responses that you can apply immediately. If you need to focus on demonstrating your ability to lead change, then you should start with the leading change scenarios.

121

Taking the time to complete the exercises will help you create action steps that lead to achieving your desired results. We encourage you to write your answers and refer to them as you prepare for leadership opportunities. At the end of this chapter, we have included recommended responses to the Ann and Alicia scenarios.

►Leadership

Over the last year, Alicia has observed Ann making the many career moves that have led to Ann becoming promotable. Initially, Alicia allowed herself to wallow in jealousy, and comparing herself to Ann. When she heard the rumors about Ann being targeted for an executive position, Alicia realized that she has to take responsibility for getting her own career goals back on track.

☐ **Describe three actions Alicia can immediately take to reposition herself.**

1. _____

_____

2. _____

_____

3. _____

_____

You have decided to either hone your leadership skills or volunteer your skills outside of the work environment.

☐ **What leadership skills can you offer a community association or your church? Why would they value what you have to offer?**

1. _____

_____

2. _____

_____

3. _____

_____

▪Communication

As a result of conducting a feedback process, Alicia has discovered that her communication style is considered abrasive by her peers and ineffective by her staff.

☐ **What steps should Alicia take to validate and correct the deficiencies?**

_____

_____

_____

_____

_____

In your quest to become a leader you have discovered that the communication style you use and observe at work is not valued within community organizations and church.

☐ **What steps should you take to learn how to effectively communicate in these environments?**

_____

_____

_____

_____

· ►►People Development

One of Alicia's supervisors is not being a team player. He gets good results but his focus is only on how he can achieve individual recognition. During their staff meetings, he tunes out when the other supervisors are giving their recap of monthly results. During his time to speak, he is articulate, organized, and engaging.

☐ **What steps should Alicia take to assist this supervisor with developing more awareness on how his behaviors are affecting the team?**

_____

_____

_____

_____

_____

You have been assigned as the chairperson for the annual community association fundraiser. Your team members attend the meetings but do not offer contributions to ensure the success of the fundraiser. You are doing all of the work. When you meet with them to discuss the problem, you learn that they are unsure about how to contribute.

☐ **What steps should you take to develop your team?**

_____

_____

_____

_____

_____

►Team Building

Ann and Alicia's teams are in competition for the annual recognition for most improved department. Ann's team has rallied around her leadership and appears to be focused on winning the competition. Alicia's team continues to show signs of being dysfunctional as a group.

☐ **What team building steps should Alicia immediately take?**

_____

_____

_____

_____

_____

You are a new female senior vice president of the company. The other five members of the executive team are males and have been with the company for about ten years. They are vice presidents who report to you. Your boss is very supportive of you but hasn't worked with a female at your level in the company.

☐ **What are the top three steps that you should take to begin to build a strong team?**

1. _____

_____

2. _____

_____

3. _____

_____

Leveraging Diversity

Alicia has the opportunity to lead a team in strategically marketing a new product line. Her success could position the Company as the leader in this field, and will provide a significant bonus for her and members of her team. In a memo from her boss, the Executive Vice President, potential team members are mentioned. There is very little diversity in the team he is considering. Alicia is scheduled to meet with him next Monday about the assignment.

☐ **What are the top three actions she should take in preparation for the meeting to ensure her concern of having a diverse team is addressed?**

1. _____

2. _____

_____

3. _____

_____

Recently a new person joined your community group. She has just moved to the neighborhood and has two children attending the local elementary school. You and other committee members are uncomfortable because her approach is very different from everyone else's. Her ideas don't seem to fit the norm. Besides, your school PTA members have worked together the last two years and are doing a fairly good job. As the newly elected president of the Parent Teachers Association (PTA), you want to lead the group to a higher level of success, and make working together a win-win relationship for both the new member and old members.

☐ **What are the top three action steps that you should take?**

1. _____

_____

2. _____

_____

3. _____

_____

*▶Leading Change

Alicia has refocused and sees an opportunity to make a difference in her organization. She has created sound strategies on how her department could significantly impact sales if a few changes were made in her department's operations. Alicia's boss is a well-respected senior vice president and isn't necessarily interested in making changes in the department.

☐ **What are the top three steps that she should take to get her ideas on the table and accepted?**

1. _____

_____

2. _____

_____

3. _____

_____

You have been giving a lot of consideration to relocating to another city. You, your husband, your children, and your extended family have lived in the same city for at least two generations that you know about. You have worked for the same company for the last twelve years, and recently learned that the company will be downsizing within the next twelve to eighteen months. You also know that although your husband is very successful in his current position, there will be some significant changes at his company over the next two years.

☐ **What are the top three steps that you should take to get your husband to consider exploring possibilities in another city?**

1. _____

_____

2. _____

_____

3. _____

_____

Recommended responses to the Ann and Alicia scenarios

There is no single right answer to the Ann and Alicia scenarios. We have, however, provided recommended responses.

· ►Leadership

Over the last year, Alicia has observed Ann making the many career moves that have led to Ann becoming promotable. Initially, Alicia allowed herself to wallow in jealousy and comparing herself to Ann. When she heard the rumors about Ann being targeted for an executive position, Alicia realized that she has to take responsibility for getting her own career goals back on track. Describe three actions Alicia can immediately take to reposition herself.

Actions

1. Select three or four colleagues who are familiar with her work performance and whose opinion she trusts and respects.

2. Ask these colleagues to be very candid about her work performance and interactions. Alicia must be prepared to listen, make no excuses, and thank her colleagues for their candid feedback.

3. She should then immediately develop a written plan for improving those areas that she thinks are most important in helping her reach her leadership goals.

· ►Communication

As a result of conducting a feedback process, Alicia has discovered that her communication style is considered abrasive by her peers and ineffective by her staff. What steps should Alicia take to correct the deficiencies?

Actions

1. Alicia needs to clearly understand what the behaviors are and begin to make the changes that she can make now.

2. Alicia needs to identify someone in her peer group who will give her feedback when she is communicating inappropriately, and set up time within the next two-four weeks to get feedback from her staff on her improved communication skills.

3. Alicia needs to talk with the human resources department about a workshop or course on effective communication.

►People Development

One of Alicia's supervisors is not being a team player. He gets good results but his focus is only on how he can achieve individual recognition. During their staff meetings, he tunes out when the other supervisors are giving their recap of monthly results. During his time to speak, he is articulate, organized, and engaging. What steps should Alicia take to assist this supervisor with developing more awareness on how his behaviors are affecting the team?

Actions

1. Alicia needs to have a private discussion with this supervisor about the observed behavior.

2. She talks with the supervisor about the importance of being a team player, obtains information from him on how he sees himself in the group, and explains her expectations.

3. She gets agreement from him on how his behavior will change. They schedule a follow up meeting to celebrate the success.

►Team Building

Ann and Alicia's teams are in competition for the annual recognition for most improved department. Ann's team has rallied around her leadership and appears to be focused on winning the competition.

Alicia's team continues to show signs of be being dysfunctional as a group. What team building steps should Alicia immediately take?

Actions

1. Alicia should assess her behavior to determine if she is demonstrating the behavior necessary as a leader.

2. If she is demonstrating the appropriate leadership behavior, then Alicia should schedule a team building session with all of her team members present. The focus of the meeting should be on the value of each member of the team and what each person brings to the table. She should ask the team what she can do to assist them in their goals.

3. Alicia needs to be sure all members understand the goals, their individual roles, and their agreed upon plan for getting there.

4. Alicia needs to make sure that she stays in touch with her team and is giving them regular feedback on how the team is performing.

5. If Alicia is not demonstrating the behavior necessary as a leader, she needs to determine the behaviors to change and then proceed immediately to make the changes.

·►Leveraging Diversity

Alicia has the opportunity to lead a team in strategically marketing a new product line. Her success could position the Company as the leader in this field, and will provide a significant bonus for her and members of her team. In a memo from her boss, the Executive Vice President, potential team members are mentioned. There is very little diversity on the team he is considering. Alicia is scheduled to meet with him next Monday about the assignment. What are the top three actions she should take in preparation for the meeting to ensure her concern of having a diverse team is addressed?

Actions

1. Alicia needs to thoroughly research the desired customer market for the new product line including the diversity of that market.

2. She needs to be prepared to present the diversity impact information including the value of team diversity in developing the best marketing strategy. This step assures the right message and a visible message about the importance of diversity is communicated.

3. Alicia needs to be prepared to make this diversity message one that is viewed as a business imperative with diversity being very broadly defined. The best method to accomplish this task is to use her fact based research documentation.

►Leading Change

Alicia has refocused and sees an opportunity to make a difference in her organization. She has created sound strategies on how her department could significantly impact sales if a few changes were made in her department's operations. Alicia's boss is a well-respected senior vice president and isn't necessarily interested in changing the focus of the department. What are the top three steps that she should take to get her ideas on the table, and accepted?

Actions

1. Alicia prepares a written proposal with an executive summary. The proposal includes her proposed strategic plan with: 1) a brief background statement, 2) recommended strategies, 3) impact (pro and con) of the strategies on people, products, processes, and equipment, 4) timeline for implementation, and 5) costs.

2. Alicia meets with her boss to present her proposal. Alicia should use audio-visual aids, if appropriate. If he says yes, she moves on with the plans.

3. If he says no, she broaches the subject of following up at a specific future date.

Chapter Eight:

Putting All The Pieces Together

L eadership is an ongoing journey. The leadership journey we have taken with you in this book has now come full circle. We believe it is important for more women to choose to lead because of all the talent and skills we have to offer. Yet, the decision to lead is an individual choice. It is our sincere hope that this book has helped you create or refine your leadership mosaic. Creating your next steps or patterns of leadership can often be a time of reckoning. Reckoning with the past, and dealing with your present reality. The past is done. Focus on the lessons learned, and try not to repeat your mistakes. Your present reality is the foundation on which to build the future. The creation of your future is in your control.

This chapter is about taking everything provided in this book and combining it with your concerted effort and focused work to help you reach your leadership goals. Its purpose is to help you bring life to the leadership advice, tools, strategies, success tips and stories that you have been reading.

One of the best ways to do that is to have you respond in writing to the questions below. Writing the responses helps you crystallize your thoughts. When your responses are in writing, you will also be able to put the information in places where you can refer to it on a regular basis. Tape it inside the medicine cabinet in your bathroom and refer to it daily. Put it in your electronic or paper personal planner so that you will see it daily. Wherever it can be a reminder to you is where you want it.

Personal Assessment

1. What are my strengths?

_____

_____

_____

_____

_____

2. Can I articulate what I offer in the area of leadership and how my skills can benefit others in ninety seconds?

☐ **Yes**
☐ **No**

If the answer is **Yes**, start practicing your pitch with people in your inner circle to obtain feedback on how you can achieve even more clarity with your message.

If the answer is **No**, take the time to create and refine your message before you approach anyone about your ability to lead.

3. What are the leadership competencies that I need to improve?

_____

_____

_____

_____

4. What steps will I take to improve these competencies?

_____

_____

_____

_____

_____

5. Am I comfortable with taking risks to achieve my leadership goals?

☐ **Yes**
☐ **No**

If the answer is **Yes**, determine an acceptable level of boldness for the environment you wish to thrive in and go for it!

If the answer is **No**, determine why you are uncomfortable with going out of your comfort zone. Once you are armed with this information, determine if the slow and steady approach will get you to your personal and professional goals in the desired timeframe. No matter what, be comfortable in your approach to displaying leadership to ensure you will be authentic in your efforts.

6. Am I willing to give up some of my personal time to create the leadership role I desire?

☐ **Yes**
☐ **No**

If the answer is **Yes**, take the time to determine a reasonable amount of personal time you can give towards creating your leadership journey without compromising your other responsibilities and other interests. Start with small chunks of dedicated time, such as one hour a day, as you move towards building your leadership strategy.

If the answer is **No**, first determine if your desire to display leadership is sincere or are you just caught up in the excitement of gaining visibility. Second, determine how you can fit your quest to be an effective leader into your existing lifestyle. Committing fifteen minutes during your lunch break to consider your next steps is an option to help you move forward.

7. What are my top priorities? In other words, what matters most to me?
   ☐ **Personal**

   _____

   _____

   _____

   _____

   _____

   ☐ **Professional/Career**

   _____

   _____

   _____

   _____

   _____

8. Why is it important to me to lead?

   _____

   _____

   _____

   _____

   _____

9. Have I had experience leading?

☐ **Yes**

☐ **No**

If the answer is Yes,

☒ Focus on the current needs and create action steps to propel the organization or culture to the next level of performance.

☒ Conduct personal assessments to determine how you can be a more effective leader.

☒ Identify an individual you can develop and help to succeed.

☒ Create an appropriate amount of down time to ensure your quest to demonstrate more leadership is in balance.

☒ Continue to execute your current leadership role at an outstanding level as you seek ways to build upon your experience.

If the answer is No,

☒ Determine the leadership environment in which you aspire to excel.

☒ Seek to learn as much as possible about the organizational culture in your chosen environment. Who are the current leaders? Assess their leadership style. Who are the worker bees? Are they motivated and productive?

☒ Assess the leadership skills you offer. Are you an outstanding communicator? Do you know how to lead teams to achieve high performance results? Do you know how to lead a meeting that produces results?

☒ Determine if the chosen environment values the leadership skills you offer.

☒ Share your aspirations with people you trust to gain support as well as to receive helpful critiques of your approach.

☒ Meet with the decision makers within the environment to determine if there is synergy to build a relationship.

10. In what arena do I want to lead?
- ☐ In my community
- ☐ In my church
- ☐ On my job
- ☐ In government/politics—local, city, state, national
- ☐ On the local school board
- ☐ In my own company—start up or ongoing
- ☐ Philanthropic organization
- ☐ Other _____

11. In what leadership position am I interested?
- ☐ President/CEO
- ☐ Department head
- ☐ Vice President
- ☐ Director
- ☐ Secretary
- ☐ Assistant Secretary
- ☐ Manager
- ☐ Committee chairperson
- ☐ Other _____

Goal Setting / Action Plan Development

1. List four leadership goals. Be specific and realistic about the goal. Remember, indicate dates for reaching the goals. And finally, be sure to prioritize the goals.

_____

_____

_____

_____

_____

2. Who will play a key role in helping me reach my leadership goals?

_____

_____

_____

_____

3. What are my action plans for reaching the leadership goals? Be specific and realistic about the action plans. Remember, indicate dates for completing the actions, and prioritize the actions. And finally, be sure my actions support the goals in response to question one above.

_____

_____

_____

_____

4. What are some obstacles that I might encounter?

_____

_____

_____

_____

5. How will I overcome the obstacles?

_____

_____

_____

_____

6. How will I track progress toward reaching my goals?

_____

_____

_____

_____

7. How will I know when I have achieved my goals?

_____

_____

_____

_____

8. How will I reward myself for achieving my goals?

_____

_____

_____

_____

It's time for you to look into the future. Once you have answered the next question, follow the same eight steps used above. For your convenience we have added some note pages in the back of this book, please refer to page IX, so that all your information will be located in one place for later reference.

9. In what arena(s) do I want to lead in five years?
   ☐ In my community
   ☐ In my church
   ☐ On my job
   ☐ In politics—village, city, state, national
   ☐ On the local school board
   ☐ In my own company—start up or ongoing
   ☐ Philanthropic organization

Now that you have completed your personal assessment you should feel comfortable that you know what you do best and where you want to begin or continue your leadership journey. Developing the goals and action plans lays the foundation for your successful leadership journey. It also puts you far ahead of most people with whom you will be working. Remember execution, execution, execution. Do what your plan calls for and when your plan calls for doing it. Your plan is not in concrete. At some point, you may decide to change or modify your direction. It may even become necessary, due to unforeseen happenings, to change or modify your goals and related plans. If so, do it. You will be consciously making the decision to modify direction and/or completion date. You are leading your life. You are weaving your leadership mosaic.

It is our sincere hope that you have realized that a lot of the leadership advice, tools, and strategies we have presented are universal. *Choose to Lead* has been written from women's perspectives and geared toward helping more women make the choice to lead and to develop the essential competencies for leadership. It is also geared toward helping those who lead become more effective at leading.

We encourage you to share the book or it's principles as a way of spreading the word about the importance of women choosing to lead and how they can successfully do it. We also hope that as a result of reading this book, the reader, whether it be a woman or a man, realizes the importance of nurturing and developing more women leaders.

Conclusion

Our collective experiences have provided the foundation for assisting other women in their choice to become leaders. Sharing our thoughts with you has been a blessing to us as we also continue our leadership journey.

We leave you with six proven leadership tips:

1. Know yourself. Know and lead with your strengths. Believe in yourself despite all odds — **Leadership.**

2. Build high performance, diverse teams by sharing information, decision making, and leadership — **Team Building.**

3. Include in your circle individuals who think differently from you to ensure all aspects of strategic thinking are involved — **Leveraging Diversity.**

4. Do more listening than talking when you are entering new leadership roles. Listen to what is being said as well as what is not being said. Learn the lay of the land. Seek to understand, then to be understood — **Communication.**

5. Have the courage to recommend and lead change. Be aware of the latest developments in your field and what will help your organization — **Leading Change**.

6. Make a conscious and deliberate effort to coach, mentor, and develop others — **People Development.**

Go as fast or slow as you like in choosing your leadership opportunities. **Boldly choose to lead.**

We invite you to keep in touch with us to share your progress. We would love to hear from you. See you in the winner's circle.

. . . .Our leadership journey also continues

Narmen and Deborah

Appendix

Resources

Books

Bell, Ella L.J. Edmondson, and Nkomo, Sella M. *Our Separate Ways: Black and White Women and the Struggle for Professional Identity.* Massachusetts: Harvard Business School Press, 2003.

Bossidy, Larry, and Charon, Ram. *Execution: The Discipline of Getting Things Done.* New York: Crown Business, 2002.

Bjorseth, Lillian. *Breakthrough Networking; Building Relationships That Last.* Lisle, IL: Duoforce Enterprises, Inc., 2003.

Foster, Jylla Moore. *Due North! Strengthen Your Leadership Assets.* Hinsdale, IL: Crystal Stairs, 2002.

Giovagnoli, Melissa, and Carter-Miller, Jocelyn. *Networlding: Building Relationships and Opportunities for Success.* San Francisco, CA: Jossey-Bass, Inc., 2002.

Hoskins, Michele with Williams, Jean A. *Sweet Expectations: Michele Hoskins' Recipe for Success.* Massachusetts: Adams Media, 2004.

Leduc, Sylva, and Smith, Nancy. *Women's Work: Choice, Chance or Socialization?* Calgary, Alberta: Detselig Enterprises, Ltd., 1992.

Malveaus, Dr. Julianne, and Perry Deborah, *Unfinished Business: A Democrat and a Republican Take on the 10 Most Important Issues Women Face.* New York: Berkeley Publishing Group, 2002.

Peters, Tom. *Re-imagine! Business Excellence in a Disruptive Age.* London: Dorling Kindersley Limited, 2003.

III

Women's Associations

American Business Women's Association – ABWA – an organization that brings together businesswomen of diverse organizations to provide opportunities for them to help themselves and others grow personally and professionally.
www.abwa.org

Business and Professional Women – BPW – an international leading advocate for working women that promotes equity for all women in the workplace.
www.bpwusa.org

Financial Women's Association – FWA – a leading executive organization committed to shaping leaders in business and finance with a special emphasis on the role and development of women.
www.fwa.org

National Association for Female Executives – NAFE – provides resources and services to empower its members to achieve career success and financial security.
www.nafe.com

Index

Note Pages

About the Authors

For more information about the co-authors' consulting, speaking, coaching and available workshops please contact:

FENNOY Consulting Group, Inc.
PO Box 271
Westmont, IL. 60559
1-708-784-1634
fennoycg@sbcglobal.net
www.fennoycg.com

Chambers Consulting Group, Ltd.
3108 S. Route 59, Suite 124 #305
Naperville, IL 60564
1-630-922-7127
deborah@chambersconsult.com
www.chambersconsult.com

Narmen Fennoy Hunter is President and CEO of FENNOY Consulting Group, Inc. (FCG, Inc.). The firm specializes in improving individual and organizational performance and results. Through their customized consulting, training, and coaching approaches, FCG, Inc., focuses on leadership development and organizational diversity. Narmen is a recognized consultant, coach, trainer, and professional speaker.

FENNOY Consulting Group, Inc. has a broad client base that includes Fortune 500 Corporations, educational institutions, not-for-profit organizations, and governmental entities.

Narmen has authored the published workbook *Developing a Business Plan* (1991), and is a contributing writer for University of Illinois YWCA book entitled *Women Making a Difference for 100 Years: 1884-1984* (1984).

She has made guest appearances discussing individual and organizational leadership development on *True to Yourself*™ WAIT 850AM radio show (Chicago). Narmen has co-sponsored three quarterly workshops since 2002: *Take Control of Your Life and Your Time, The Art of Networking, and Successfully Start Your Own Business.*

Narmen has served as a trustee on a community college board, Board of Director member of the Greater Chicago Arthritis Foundation, Ronald House fundraising committee member, Link Unlimited sponsor, and is a member of the media ministry of her church.

Narmen holds professional memberships in Society for Human Resource Management (SHRM), American Society for Training and Development (ASTD), International Coach Federation (ICF), and National Association for Female Executives (NAFE). She is a member of the Oak Brook Area Association of Commerce and Industry (OBAACI) and co-chairs OBAACI's Business women's Network. She is associated with Leadership Management, Inc.

Narmen has an MA degree from Washington University in St. Louis and a BA from Millikin University. She did post-graduate work at the University of Illinois-UC Labor & Industrial Relations Institute and received a Certificate in Equal Employment Opportunity (EEO) studies from Cornell University.

Photo by Leroy Hicks, Jr.

Deborah Chambers Chima is the President and CEO of Chambers Consulting Group, Ltd., a company that assists organizations with creating an environment where cohesiveness and collaboration are the catalysts for achieving greater business results. She specializes in improving organizational productivity through team building, leadership development, and customer service. She is a consultant, professional speaker, and executive coach. Before establishing her firm, Ms. Chima spent 24 years in the retail industry with the last 21 years at McDonald's Corporation, where she held various corporate management positions in international and domestic markets. Her solid base of experience and unique set of skills in Operations, Training and Development, Management, Sales and Customer Service are demonstrated in her track record of achieving award winning results.

Deborah holds professional memberships in the American Society of Training & Development (ASTD), National Speakers Association (NSA), National Association of Female Executives (NAFE), as well as the International Coach Federation (ICF). Deborah is currently working on her coach certification through Coachville School of Coaching. She is also a member of the National Association of Women Business Owners (NAWBO), and serves on the Women in Business Steering Committee with the Naperville Chamber of Commerce. An authorized distributor of Inscape Publishing's DiSC® assessments, she is passionate about helping people ignite the path that will achieve their personal and professional goals.

Ms. Chima received recognition in 2003 from Manchester Who's Who Among Executives and Professional Women for her achievements.

Deborah has served on the Board of Managers for the Martin Luther King Boy's & Girl's Club and currently serves as a Board Director for Agape Connections, Inc. She volunteers with Big Brothers/ Big Sisters of America, Zeta Phi Beta Sorority, Inc. and the Warrenville Illinois Youth Center.

Ms. Chima earned a Bachelor of Science degree in Business Administration from the University of Illinois in Champaign, Urbana.

Are You Doing All You Can To Be A Leader? This Book Will Show You The Path To Leadership!

Check with your neighborhood and online bookstores or order here.

Toll-Free: 1-866-372-2636

Secure Online Ordering www.CameoPublications.com

	#	Amount
Choose to Lead *Advice, Tools, and Strategies For Women From Women* Paperback 168pp *(ISBN 0-9744149-7-2):* **$17.95**		
Shipping USA: $4.95 for first item; add $2.00 for each additional book. Canada: $6.00 for first item; add $4.00 for each additional book.		
Order Total		

Please Print

Name _____

Company _____

Ship To _____

City/State/Zip _____ Country

Phone (   ) _____ E-mail (optional)

Cameo Publications
PO BOX 8006
Hilton Head, SC 29938

credit card # _____

please sign _____